THE MURDER OF

BRIAN JONES

THE MURDER OF

BRIAN
JONES

THE SECRET STORY
OF MY LOVE AFFAIR
WITH THE MURDERED
ROLLING STONE

ANNA WOHLIN WITH **CHRISTINE LINDSJÖÖ**

BLAKE

Published by Blake Publishing Ltd,
3 Bramber Court, 2 Bramber Road,
London W14 9PB, England

First published in 1999

ISBN 1 85782 3168

British Library Cataloguing-in-Publication Data:
A catalogue record for this book is available
from the British Library.

Typeset by BCP

Printed in Great Britain by
Creative Print and Design (Wales), Ebbw Vale, Gwent

1 3 5 7 9 10 8 6 4 2

contents

BRIAN JONES

To Amanda and Pierre

prologue

I cried in despair. I awoke in the middle of the night and wept my heart out into the darkness.

By now I have stopped crying, but my heart still weeps.

The nightmares are still my nightly companions — sometimes they visit more frequently. They have become a part of my life.

Although it is almost 30 years since Brian drowned in our swimming pool at Cotchford Farm, I still wake up in the night in a cold sweat and with a thumping heart. In my dreams, I can see Brian fall to the bottom of the pool, out of my reach. I keep ducking down into the water, trying to get a hold of him, but each time I push nearer he falls deeper into the dark, abysmal depths.

In my dream, I see people standing around the pool watching us. I recognise a few, but not all. Beside myself, I cry out for help.

'Help me! Please, help me to save Brian!'

The spectators remain motionless. Through a haze, I can see them smile scornfully.

'Did you really think it would be this easy, Anna?' they say in chorus.

With those words the nightmare ends and I wake up, bursting into tears.

After all these years, I still do not understand what they mean. Maybe they imply that it will take a long time yet for the truth about Brian's death to be disclosed.

In the years since Brian's death, I have done my very best to repress the memories of that tragic night, denying what happened.

I have always known that I have the key to that last piece of information that, after 30 years, will help solve the mystery surrounding Brian's death.

I was intimidated into silence, but I am not scared any more.

For Brian's sake, and for that of his sons, I want to unveil the truth — while there is still time.

CHAPTER ONE

BRIAN

I returned to London two months after Brian's tragic death. Not only had I lost Brian, I had also lost our eagerly awaited child and was in a fragile state of mind.

As soon as I reached London, I got in touch with Les Perrin, who handled public relations for the Rolling Stones. When I was forced to leave England within a week of Brian's death, he had promised to find an apartment for me if I decided to return to London.

His voice betrayed him. He was not at all pleased that I was back in London. But he recovered from the initial shock of hearing my voice and remembered his promise, asking me to stay in a hotel while he tried to find me a more permanent home. And he assured me that he would take care of the bill.

Looking back, I am sure that Allan Klein, the Rolling Stones' manager, Les Perrin and the band's tour manager, Tom Keylock, were convinced that they had given me such a scare that they would never see or hear from me again. But I could not stay away.

I was restless and anxious and I felt that my only reason to go on living was to tell the truth surrounding Brian's death. I just didn't know how to go about it.

*   *   *

On my return to London, I decided to go to see Alexis Korner, one of Brian's oldest and closest friends. Alexis is probably better known for his R&B club in Ealing and the gifted musicians he discovered than for the music they made in his band, but in those days he was a well-known and well-respected musician. Brian loved him both as a friend and as a musician, and the two of them had been planning a tour in Germany just before Brian's death.

Alexis, his wife Bobbie and their children had visited Brian and me at Cotchford Farm on several occasions after Brian's split from the Stones, and they always received me with open arms.

I was deeply touched by their sympathy and their support and more than ever I understood why Brian had always praised them. They were friends, genuine friends. They were there for you when you needed them and they never asked for anything in return.

During my first weeks in London, I looked up my old friends and I paid frequent visits to the Stones' office. They were all polite and cordial, but not overly friendly. I wanted somebody to care, to talk about Brian, to listen to me and maybe even console me, but it was a forlorn hope.

I knew in my heart that they didn't want me around. I realised this when I talked to Les Perrin a few days after my arrival and he, somewhat uneasily, reluctantly admitted that he had not fulfilled his original promise to help me. But I couldn't help myself. I was drawn to the office. It was my last link with Brian.

*   *   *

My return to London attracted attention and suddenly I was the toast of the town. Everybody wanted my company. Overnight, I was a well-known face. I was special. I was Brian Jones' girlfriend, the girl who had been with him on the night he died.

At first I was flattered on account of those strangers who apparently cared for me. I thought it was nice to receive a variety of invitations and all that attention. But I soon realised that I had misinterpreted their motives.

I was not used to these types of people. I was naïve and thought that they really cared for me and wanted to help me get on with my life. To my great disappointment, it was not long before I understood that my new found friends only used me and my new status.

At the same time, I discovered that the only thing we had in common was drugs. I fought to survive and it was easy to deaden the pain with drugs. They helped me to escape and suppress my grief — at least, for a while.

Soon after my arrival in London, I remember writing a letter to Mick Jagger. I don't recall my exact words, but I believe I, among other things, accused him of not caring enough about Brian's death. I take it that Mick didn't like the letter. He never wrote back.

Now and then I thought about seeing Mick and talking to him face to face, and one night I suddenly spotted him at the Speakeasy, a rock club in London which was owned by my very good friend Jim Carter-Fea.

The Speakeasy was the in-place for people who moved in creative circles. The club was a rendezvous for journalists, writers, photographers, artists, actors and musicians who flocked there to chat and listen to music played by the aspiring new bands.

The club was a little more sophisticated than the Marquee, which was the most popular rock club in those days, with its dark red colours and stylish décor. It seemed more like a nightclub than a rock club, but the atmosphere was the same as in the Marquee and the sound levels were almost as loud as in all the other rock clubs in London. I always enjoyed going there.

Mick looked up at me but I am not sure that he recognised me. We didn't know each other and we had never been properly introduced, even though we had met at the Stones' office. Today, I regret that I didn't approach him, but at the time it just didn't seem like a good idea.

I remember thinking that it was terribly unfair seeing Mick alive and thriving. It almost broke my heart. He was a reminder that he and all the other members of the Stones were still continuing as if nothing had happened, while Brian was gone. For ever.

But at the same time, I would have liked to have known how the Rolling Stones were holding up, how they felt having lost a good friend, how they were coping with their grief. I wanted to know how they remembered Brian, if they just talked about his bad points, or if they remembered him when he was at his best. I also wanted to know if they missed him, if their lives were emptier without him. I had a host of questions, questions which are still unanswered.

My thoughts revolved around Brian, day and night. I knew in my heart that I could not go any further towards healing until I had laid the ghosts surrounding Brian's death to rest.

I told my closest friends about the events that led up to the tragedy and they urged me to go to the police and tell them what had really happened at Cotchford Farm on the night of the 2nd and 3rd of July 1969.

I wanted to take their advice, but my constant fear of reprisals prevented me from doing so. I simply didn't know what would happen to me if I told the truth. Maybe I would share Brian's fate.

*   *   *

When I was leaving the Stones' office one afternoon I met Brian's father, Lewis Jones. He put his arm around me and asked me how I felt.

'I miss Brian so badly,' I sobbed, 'I still can't accept that he's gone.'

Lewis gave me a comforting hug and we stood in silence for a moment.

'I missed you at the funeral,' Lewis said. 'I expected you to be there when Brian was finally laid to rest.'

My eyes welled with tears. 'I know,' I said. 'I wanted to, but I couldn't.'

Lewis' sympathy and understanding made me burst into tears. I didn't know how to explain why I hadn't attended the funeral. I couldn't tell him that it wasn't my choice. I didn't want to burden him any further.

To my relief, Lewis didn't ask.

'Maybe it was just as well that you didn't come,' he said sadly. 'It was beautiful in the church and I was touched to see that Brian was loved by so many strangers, but the funeral turned into total chaos.

'It was a strange feeling. Brian suddenly belonged to the world and I felt like an outsider. I had wanted to bid him a quiet farewell but it was impossible. The church and the streets in Cheltenham were crowded with people.

'I am glad we met,' he continued. 'There is so much I want to talk to you about. I have tried to get in touch with you, but no one in the office knew where I could find you.'

'I've been in Stockholm,' I said. 'I just got back a couple of weeks ago.'

'Did you visit Cotchford Farm before you left?' Lewis asked.

'No. I wanted to, but I wasn't allowed. I am thinking about going down and collecting my stuff, but I don't know if I have the strength.'

'Anna, I'm sorry to have to tell you,' Lewis said, taking my hand, 'but there is nothing left in the house. Everything's gone. Brian's clothes, albums, tapes, musical instruments, Gobelain tapestry ... That's one of the reasons I wanted to talk to you. I was hoping you could tell me what has happened to Brian's belongings.'

Bewildered, I stared at Lewis, trying desperately to think thing's through. What about my private property, the clothes Brian gave me, my letters, my camera and everything else?

'But ... my things? Are they gone, too?'

'Yes,' Lewis replied. 'When we arrived, the house was empty. We couldn't find any trace of Brian's personal possessions and I didn't see anything of yours. Everything's gone and nobody knows who cleaned the house out. Whoever it was took the lot — even the sheets!'

I couldn't believe it. Why should anyone rob the house? Who would want our private belongings? How could anyone be so cruel to us?

I was shocked. It was the first time I heard that the house had been cleared out. Later, I heard rumours to the effect that some of the workmen had emptied the house. They were said to have loaded our possessions on to lorries and that they had burnt anything they didn't want. I suppose my clothes and personal belongings had ended up on that bonfire, too.

Before meeting Lewis, I had thought that everything would

be exactly as I had left it and I was planning on returning to collect my personal belongings as soon as I felt up to it.

It broke my heart when I looked into Lewis' eyes. I felt so sorry for him. It was distressing for me, but for Lewis and Louise, Brian's mother, it must have been so much worse. Brian was their second child to have been taken from them at a young age. The grief must have been unspeakable.

I didn't know how to comfort him. I squeezed his hand and we just stood in silence for a moment.

'I want you to know that Brian was happy,' I said. 'We were planning our future and he was very excited and optimistic.'

'I know,' Lewis said. 'We spoke on the phone a couple of days before he died and I could tell that he was in good spirits. I was very happy for him and the shock was even greater when I got the news about his drowning.

'I couldn't believe it. Brian was an excellent swimmer and I still can't understand how he drowned.'

'You mustn't believe what they say or write in the papers,' I said. 'Brian was neither drunk nor under the influence of any drugs.'

'I believe you,' Lewis said and pulled out a photo from the inside pocket of his jacket.

'Anna, I want you to have this.' He held it out for me.

The black-and-white picture shows Brian when he was about five years old. He is standing outside his family home dressed in a shirt, a pair of shorts with braces, knee socks and shoes. He is the epitome of a smiling, flaxen-haired child with no worries in the world. Tears flooded into my eyes again.

'Anna, nobody can take our memories away from us. Let's cherish our memories of Brian.'

Lewis told me that I was welcome to visit him and his wife whenever I wanted. They were there for me, if I needed them.

We said goodbye, but his words lingered in my thoughts.

Could it really be possible that all our things had gone?

I felt a strong urge to go back to Cotchford Farm. But I couldn't. Not yet. It was too early.

*   *   *

Over the following months, I did my best to get on with my life. With the help of Alexis, I moved into a small apartment and started to work again. In the evenings, I went out with my friends and tried to enjoy myself.

I never discussed Brian or our life together with my friends. I repressed my thoughts of him and tried to convince myself that my boyfriend was not the same man as the one people were gossiping about.

And he wasn't. My Brian was a thriving, radiantly happy, charming man with sparkling eyes and a winning smile who loved his new life in the country.

The Brian people talked about was a worn-out, depressed and lonely pot-head.

I slept with Brian's shirts nearby to keep his scent near me and he returned to me in my dreams. The memories of the horrible weeks following Brian's death tormented me and when spring came I knew it was no longer possible to put off my visit to the farm. I had to get on with my life and I needed to go there to regain my strength; not only to see if Lewis was right about the house having been cleared, but also because Brian constantly talked to me in my dreams, begging me to clear his name.

'Anna, you must tell everybody that I didn't drown. You must tell them what really happened!'

The only way I could agree to Brian's wishes was to try to draw strength at Cotchford Farm, the home I shared with him. Maybe a visit to the house would give me the courage to speak the truth.

But I was alone in a foreign country and I had signed a contract prohibiting me from giving any interviews regarding Brian's life or death without permission from Les Perrin at Rolling Stones Incorporated. I wasn't sure what would happen to me if I decided to talk to a journalist without his approval. I feared that I might be sued, or worse, and I had no money to cover a law suit or damages.

Neither did I know what might happen to me if I talked to the police. Could it be as bad as talking to the press?

*   *   *

In May 1970, the time had come to visit Cotchford Farm. I couldn't face going alone, so I took an acquaintance with me for the journey. I was trembling all over when we boarded the train at Victoria Station. I felt permanently guilty that I had not fought harder to expose the truth about Brian and clear his name. And I had also allowed others to take control of my life and left it to them to decide what I should or shouldn't do.

I know that Brian would have acted differently. If anything had happened to me, he would have stood his ground until the truth had been revealed. He would never have tolerated being pushed around by others or being threatened, I am quite sure of that.

When we arrived at East Grinstead late in the afternoon, I was a bundle of nerves, and they grew worse as we sat in a taxi on our way to the farmhouse. When the car reached the private lane, I asked the driver to stop. I wanted to walk down to the house on my own. I stepped out of the taxi and looked at the house where Brian's builder, Frank Thorogood, had lived. Then I slowly made my way down towards my former home. My legs almost gave way when I saw the house and I suddenly regretted the trip.

I don't know what I had expected, but certainly not the feeling of tension and depression that engulfed me. When I had lived in the house there had always been a bustling throng everywhere; now the house stood abandoned and silent. There were no voices, no barking, not even birdsong. It was almost unbearably still.

My heart broke when I approached the house, which I had come to love almost as much as Brian had loved it, and where I had experienced both brimming happiness and unspeakable grief. It looked forlorn and I couldn't help but feel sorry for it. It seemed incredible that AA Milne had once written his famous stories about Winnie the Pooh in that house, stories which encapsulated the sweetness and innocence of childhood. To think that such a sense of joy surrounding this place could have been swept away by such sadness.

I didn't know then that the house had already been sold and that the new owner had not been allowed to take possession until 18 months after the purchase had been completed.

After a while I collected myself and hurried round the house to the backyard — and the swimming pool. The garden was well kept and the flowers were in bloom. I assumed that Brian's gardener, Mick Martin, still took care of it.

In spite of the beautiful garden, I could not rid myself of the feeling that the place was deserted. The feeling of sadness grew when I approached the pool.

Brian had taken great pride in his blue swimming pool, having nursed it as if it was his baby. The water was always crystal clear and Brian used to spend hours removing leaves and dirt. There was no mistaking that he enjoyed every single minute and he would not allow anyone else to attend to his pool. It was his pride and joy. And it was where he met his fate.

The pool looked as abandoned and deserted as the house. The water was dirty and the surface and the bottom were covered with debris. Brian would have burst into tears if he had seen the pool in such poor condition.

I took a deep breath and walked round it, staring down in to the dark water. Maybe I nurtured a vain hope that Brian would playfully break the surface of the dark water, as he used to, and give me one of his flashing smiles.

I raised my eyes and looked around for our dogs; Emily, Luther and the three lively puppies. I had allowed my imagination to run away with me and I half expected to see the five of them running towards me with wagging tails and happy barks. But I only heard the sound of silence.

I suddenly realised why I had put off the visit to Cotchford Farm. As long as I kept away, I could go on pretending that all that had happened was merely a bad dream, and that I would soon wake up with Brian by my side. During this first visit, the truth dawned on me.

Brian was gone. For ever. He was dead. He would never return.

My hope deserted me. I sank to my knees beside the swimming pool and cried my heart out. And the next thing I remember is Brian standing in front of me.

He smiled his irresistible smile and I found myself wrapped in unforgettable memories of our love story.

CHAPTER TWO

BRIAN

In 1962, the year Brian formed the Rolling Stones, I visited England for the first time. I was an exchange student from Sweden and I came to London to improve my English. In the daytime I studied English grammar and when the evening came I explored London's nightlife.

I was only 15, and I loved London from the start — the atmosphere, the thriving rock clubs, the music, the people. I decided to return as soon as I could.

Three years went by, during which time I was introduced to a new band called the Rolling Stones. One of my friends bought their first album and played it for me.

I was a bit snobbish and preferred the Beatles. The Stones were too saucy for my liking and their music was a little too raucous. But at the same time, they communicated something sexy and primitive that attracted me.

On my return to London 1965, I went to a huge rock concert

with my friend Lisa. I think it was in March. Different bands were playing on small stages set up within a big field, around which the audience could walk freely. The Rolling Stones were the main attraction for the night.

Since Lisa and I had arrived in London we had made a lot of new friends. Among them were the boys in the Yardbirds and the Animals and it was for their sake we went to the concert. They were still fairly unknown and they liked their friends to come and listen and scream a little to draw attention to them.

Especially for the evening I had spent my last pennies on a pair of fantastic Jaeger trousers and I caused quite a stir when I strolled around and chatted with the boys I knew. Everybody suddenly wanted to talk to Lisa and me, even boys we didn't know. It was very flattering.

Eventually, we ended up in front of the stage on which the Stones played. I listened to their music and thought that they sounded like every other band, no better and no worse than the rest. The only thing different was Brian. When I saw him, something inexplicable clicked in me.

Brian made such a strong impression on me. I felt that we belonged together. Our eyes met and my heart missed a beat, but Brian didn't approach me.

Mick Jagger did. He jumped off the stage when the Stones had played their last song and grabbed me. I told him that I wasn't interested, but he refused to let me go. Instead, he started dragging me to the exit, while the fans shouted and screamed. I hissed at him to let me go, but he didn't hear me. Finally, I had to pull myself away from him.

It was Brian's magnetic gaze that was forever stamped on my memory.

*   *   *

The rock club to go to above all others in the Sixties was the Marquee Club. This scruffy club in Soho was legendary. It was where all the new pop and rock bands took their first faltering steps to stardom. All new bands dreamed of playing at the Marquee.

The interior décor was nothing to boast about. It was plain and ordinary, consisting of simple tables and chairs and almost non-existent lighting.

But there was a wonderful atmosphere. At the Marquee you could meet established musicians as well as hopeful newcomers. The club was noisy and boisterous and you almost had to cut your way through the heavy smoke. Hashish had become an unofficial fixture of London's night life. Joints were carefully slipped in and out of different hands under the tables. I made friends with a lot of people and I soon felt at home there.

The Stones visited the club from time to time, but during my first years in London they were touring a great deal. The first time I saw Brian at the club was in 1966. The Stones had recently returned to London after touring Australia and Europe, and Brian and I had passed each another in Bond Street a couple of days before. We had still not talked, but every fibre of my body was stimulated when our eyes met. It was a magical attraction and I knew that Brian felt its force as well.

Brian saw me as soon as he entered the club; my bright yellow trousers were hard to miss, but I didn't notice him. I had my back to the entrance and was a bit annoyed when Lisa suddenly pushed me without warning.

'Brian's on his way over,' she hissed in my ear and my irritation evaporated.

My heart started to pound and I felt my cheeks flush, but I didn't dare to turn round and before he reached us a couple of fans saw him and started to scream.

I turned in time to see Brian rushing out of the club. Privately,

I cursed the fans for not leaving him in peace.

*   *   *

I was deeply attracted to Brian for several reasons, one of which was his fantastic dress sense. He had class, but at the same time he dared to appear in public in the most wonderful outfits. I felt that he was a kindred spirit, as interested in outrageous and sensational clothes as I was. We both liked to stick out from the crowd and mix glaring colours with multicoloured patterns. We both had clear ideas about our overall look and we were not afraid to carry them out. I had never before met a man with such a pronounced interest in clothes and fashion. Brian fascinated me like no man had done before.

I admired his creative style and the combination of elegance and decadence. He was very special and I knew in my heart that we were a match made in heaven.

In the Sixties, London seemed a much smaller place, and Brian and I ran into one another now and then. Usually, it was in Bond Street, which he passed through on his way to the Stones' office. The electricity between us was almost tangible.

Brian's magnetism and charisma eclipsed everyone around him. Even if the street was crowded, he was the only one who attracted my attention.

I followed his career in the papers and I read about his relationship with the German model Anita Pallenberg. I could not stop myself. I was jealous and miserable when I thought about them together. She was beautiful and she was famous. I was convinced that Brian had met the woman with whom he would stay for the rest of his life. But I could not get him out of my system. He was the man of my dreams. My first true love.

But despite Brian's girlfriend, I still felt the attraction between us when we met in the streets or in the clubs. I also knew deep in my heart that Brian felt exactly the same way.

*   *   *

Lisa and I had a good time almost every night and we became acquainted with many well-known people and musicians who were gradually cruising towards stardom. One of our struggling friends was the now-famous singer Rod Stewart.

I remember how we used to make fun of Rod because he could never resist the urge to check his hair in every shop window he passed. He was a short, slender boy and his blond haircut was very much the same as it is today. It always reminded me of a hedgehog.

Rod sang at a club in Hampstead and he was struggling to get a record deal. He wanted to be somebody, and his stubbornness eventually paid off. But in those days even he had a hard time getting invitations to the clubs in London as most of them required you to be a member.

Lisa and I had no trouble getting past the doormen, partly because we knew them, partly because of our wild outfits, and Rod constantly nagged us to take him with us. Now and then we felt sorry for him and agreed, but always on one condition; he had to follow at least a couple of yards behind us because we were ashamed of his worn-out shoes. Rod accepted this and he shuffled along behind like a faithful puppy.

We got to know Jimi Hendrix and remained friends with the Yardbirds and the Animals. Lisa fell in love with Jeff Beck and for a while they dated. I met a fashion photographer, Sean, and consoled myself with him.

It was natural for Lisa and me to spend most of our time with creative, artistic types, but we also made friends with a lot of aristocrats, and were often invited to weekends in the country, fox-hunting or partying. We were young, we were curious and we just wanted to have fun.

In the winter of 1966, Lisa and I went back to Sweden. Lisa felt homesick, and I decided to go with her. I spent a year in Sweden, travelling around the country with the go-go dance group The Ravens, and appeared with the group on the TV show *Popside*. It was a hectic and fun year, but I longed to return to London. And when I did, I was hoping it would be for good.

*   *   *

In the spring of 1967, I met Brian at the Speakeasy. I had not seen him for more than a year, and I felt a bit nervous when I saw him sitting in the middle of a group of friends. He looked up and smiled when he noticed me. Then he stood up, walked towards me and, for the first time, we talked.

'Hello,' he said. 'I'm Brian. What's your name?'

'Anna,' I answered, my heart pounding.

'You aren't from here, are you?'

'No, I'm Swedish,' I said.

'What're you doing in England?'

'Working, on and off.'

'Have you made any plans for tonight?' he asked. 'If not, we could go to my place.'

I couldn't help but notice that he was drunk and I pretended not to be interested, although my heartbeat was probably visible through my blouse.

'No,' I said. 'I don't think that's a good idea.'

Brian started to say something, but was interrupted by Jim Carter-Fea who approached us. The three of us started to chat, but after a while Brian excused himself and returned to his friends.

I casually glanced at him during the evening and got the feeling that he wasn't all there, that he was lonely in spite of all the people who crowded him. But I wasn't interested in his problems. The time wasn't right for us.

I was proud that I had had the strength to turn him down, but I was certain that one day we would be together. I wanted him, but I didn't want to end up as one of his hunting trophies.

Brian and I later discussed what happened that evening.

'I wanted you and you wanted me,' he said. 'Why did you turn me down? I still don't understand it.'

'It didn't feel right,' I said. 'I didn't want to be a one-night-stand.'

'Oh yeah? Are you sure that's what would have happened?'

I shrugged my shoulders.

'OK,' he said, smiling sheepishly, 'I suppose I respected you for turning me down — even if it didn't make any sense.'

*   *   *

A year later, in the autumn of 1968, Brian and I ran into each other again at a private party. I knew by then that Anita had left him to live with Keith Richards and during the year the Rolling Stones had also made the headlines over their link with drugs. Mick and Keith were the first to get busted and, later the same year, Brian was arrested for possession of cannabis and for allowing his flat to be used for smoking joints.

I had heard that Brian was deeply depressed about his break-up with Anita. Rumour had it that his feeling of betrayal, in combination with the bust, had made him suicidal. I'd also heard on the grapevine that Brian was seeing the model Suki Poiter and I hoped for his sake that he was feeling better.

I arrived at the party with a good friend. We had decided to drop in on our way to Speakeasy. I didn't know that Brian was supposed to be there and it was a bit of a shock to see him again.

'Hello!' he crooned when I passed him and his friends. He

turned to his companions.

'This is Anna from Sweden,' he said. 'I think she'll turn me down.'

I didn't know what to say and his friends started to tease him.

'Hello ... how are you?' I couldn't think of anything else to say.

'Stoned out of my head!' he answered cheerfully. And I knew he was only kidding.

My friend took me to one side.

'Brian is a bad choice,' he said. 'He is too self-centred and egotistical. For your own good, you should steer clear.'

I didn't respond. A little annoyed, I'd have preferred him to mind his own business, but I reluctantly left the party in his company.

When I got home later that night, I cursed myself for not having stayed, and taken a risk with Brian.

*   *   *

As usual, I spent Christmas with my family in Sweden, and I took the opportunity to visit my friends. I still remember one night as vividly as if it had happened yesterday.

I was visiting one of my girlfriends and we where chatting about this and that. At one point, she asked me if I had a boyfriend in London and before I could stop myself I said, 'Yes, I'm seeing Brian Jones ... you know ... the Rolling Stone.'

A second later, I wished the ground would open up and swallow me, but my girlfriend looked impressed and I was to ashamed to tell her that I'd lied.

I didn't know why I said that Brian was my boyfriend. I still wish that I'd had the courage to take it back. My behaviour made me deeply ashamed. Looking back, I can't help but wonder if it was a portent of what was going to happen when I got back to London.

THE MEETINGS

*   *   *

In late January 1969, I was invited to a party. I had been told that Brian had also been invited, but no one knew whether he'd be there.

I was chatting at the party with a couple of friends when a gentle murmur went round the room. I turned and saw Brian come in. My body tingled. My friends chattered on, but I couldn't hear their words. All my attention was focused on Brian and I wondered if anything would happen between us that night. Or, God forbid, what if he didn't see me?

The women at the party were all beautiful and I suddenly felt very insecure. I had done my best to look as attractive as possible and had chosen a gorgeous white crocheted gown and luscious lace underwear, which was just visible through the dress.

Brian occasionally glanced at me over the following hour and each time it felt as intense as a laser beam. I tried to be attentive to my friends, but it was hard to concentrate knowing that Brian was so close. We were both aware of each other and the world ground to a halt each time our eyes met. I felt sure that he was going to come over to me before too long.

That particular evening, I learned the depth of Brian's unique attraction. His charisma made him the object of everyone's attention, and when he entered the room you couldn't help but be drawn to him.

Brian wasn't the only celebrity at the party. Peter Sellers, David Niven Jr and Roman Polanski were among the other famous guests. But Brian was special and was soon swamped by both men and women. I found him both exciting and dangerous.

I stopped to have a chat with David Niven Jr. We were friends and had seen a great deal of each other during my years in

London. I was very fond of him and I still have a gift which he presented me with one day — an alarm clock! I sometimes found it difficult to get to places on time and, in the nicest of ways, he found a way of pointing it out.

After a while I left David to go to the bar, but before I reached it I felt a hand on my back and fingers sliding their way around my waist.

'We've met before, haven't we?' a voice whispered in my ear.

I turned round and saw Brian smiling at me. I was so surprised that, if asked, I'd have been hard-pressed to remember my own name. It took me quite a while to pull myself together.

'Yes ... from time to time,' I managed to splutter.

'I want to be alone with you,' Brian said.

'Maybe,' I answered calmly, although I was trembling all over and my legs threatened to give way.

Brian took my arm and led me out of the room. He didn't stop until we stood outside the bathroom.

'I've been wanting to see you for a long time,' he said. 'I don't know anything about you except that you're Swedish. Come on, what are you doing in England? What's it like living in a foreign country? Don't you feel lonely sometimes?'

Brian fired a few more questions at me, but I couldn't answer. My tongue felt heavy in my mouth. But Brian didn't wait for an answer, he just ploughed on.

'I moved to the country,' he suddenly said. 'I've learned to appreciate the scent of dust.'

'Ashes to ashes, dust to dust ...' I said, and regretted the words as they came out.

Brian gave me a surprised look, then he started to laugh. It was infectious, and I soon joined him.

The laughter helped me relax and we chatted idly for a while. I told him that I had first come to England to study the language and that I'd enjoyed it so much I'd had to come back.

'You're a bit young to be living alone in a foreign country, aren't you?' Brian said.

'I'm 22,' I said, a bit offended. 'I can look after myself.'

'I still think you're a bit young to be on your own,' he replied, bringing the subject to a close.

During our months together, Brian often remarked on my age and lectured me on having left Sweden and my family before I'd finally grown up. I disagreed with him, but I could not change his mind. Sometimes he seemed to be more at home in a pulpit giving a sermon.

Brian told me that he had revalued his life and had begun making plans for the future.

'I'm sick and tired of the music business,' he said. 'All the drugs, the hangers-on and the groupies.'

He told me that he wanted a nice, quiet life, and that he had found a house where he wanted to raise a family and grow old.

I looked at him and imagined throwing myself into his arms. He was so handsome and gentle. But I didn't want him to think that I was an easy catch.

Brian talked me into leaving the party and we sneaked away without telling anyone. I'd decided that the time had come to give in to him. I had longed for him on and off for the last five years and now I'd finally got my chance. I'd convinced myself that I had nothing to lose, and everything to gain.

When we left the house, Brian gently put his arms around me and gave me a kiss. He caressed my cheek and mumbled something in my ear. I didn't catch what he said, and I didn't want to ruin the perfect moment. I was brimming over with happiness and wished that the night would never end.

Brian drew back after a few moments and called for a taxi. He took me to a small restaurant in Knightsbridge where nobody paid us any attention. It was the first time I'd been in a restaurant where people brought their own wine. It was as picturesque as it was romantic.

After we'd placed our orders, Brian told me about his life with the Stones. He talked about some of the tours they'd done.

'When we first started out as a band, we were flattered when the girls ran after us instead of vice versa,' he said. 'But soon we began to compete over who could bed the most girls, and we took what we could get. There were never any feelings involved and, in the end, we began to despise both the girls and ourselves.

'That time is long gone, but then we were young and hungry and we didn't realise that quality is far better than quantity.'

He was silent for a moment and then he took my hand.

'Enough about me, I want to know more about you. How long have you been in England?'

'Since 1964.'

'Do you miss Sweden?'

'No, I like it here. But I never spend Christmas here. I like being with my family when Santa Claus arrives.'

Brian asked how Christmas was different in Sweden, and I told him about the early service on Christmas Day, which we call *julotta*. I told him about the horses and the sleigh ride to the church, what we eat, and that we exchange our Christmas presents, called *julklappar*, on Christmas Eve.

'I want to spend next Christmas in Sweden,' Brian said excitedly. 'I've never had a *julklappar* on Christmas Eve!'

I laughed at him when he used the Swedish word. He repeated it several times until he got it right.

The food arrived and we began to eat, but I was too nervous to enjoy it.

'How do you support yourself?' Brian asked after a while. 'Are you working?'

'Yes ... in a shop ... selling clothes,' I told him. 'But it's just a temporary job. It's hard to get a permanent one. I've worked in a few different shops, in a hotel, as a maid and even an au-pair, but that didn't last long. So far, I've done OK.'

'What about your residence permit?'

'That's always a problem. But I ask one of my friends to certify that I work for her — or him.'

I could tell that Brian wasn't impressed. He shook his head and groaned.

'If I ever have a daughter, I won't allow her to leave England before her 25th birthday!'

He wanted to know more about my life in England and I told him what I'd been doing: how I'd once accepted help from a stranger who'd offered me a place to stay ('How could you? You didn't know him!'); how I always hitch-hiked to save money ('I don't believe it ... do you have any idea what could happen to you?') and other things. Brian was horrified.

I thought he was exaggerating his concern and couldn't understand why he was so upset. I was young and naïve and I never thought twice about the consequences.

Today, I understand Brian. We all grow older and wiser.

*   *   *

A friend of mine had offered me somewhere to stay while I was searching for a new apartment and when I got back that night my head was spinning. I hoped, wished, but didn't dare to believe, that Brian and I would finally get together. Was he fond of me or was I just one of a handful of girlfriends?

My friend noticed that something had happened and I told her I'd finally met Brian and talked to him. I think she regretted having asked me because she had to listen to me going on about him for hours. I was on cloud nine, in love and didn't fall asleep until dawn.

I went over what Brian had told me about his girlfriend, Suki Poiter.

'I'm not in love with her, but I *am* fond of her and I feel responsible for her,' Brian had said. 'She was engaged to one of my best friends, Tara Browne.'

He told me that Tara, who had been the heir to the Guinness empire, had been killed in a car accident. He'd come from a distinguished family, and in those days it was popular among the rich and powerful to associate with rock stars and Tara and Brian had become friends.

'When I heard what had happened I flew to Ireland for the funeral,' Brian continued. 'And I tried to comfort Suki over the following months.'

Brian and Anita were still a couple when Tara died and they both kept Suki company.

'After my break-up with Anita I met Suki at a party. She lived a secluded life and I felt sorry and concerned for her.'

Brian told me that Suki could never be a substitute for Anita. His relationship with Suki was based on friendship. She comforted him for his loss, and he comforted her for hers.

'She is a sweet, sad girl and I felt that I had to take care of her for Tara's sake,' Brian explained.

Brian was fond of Suki and he always wanted the best for the people he cared about. If he could do something to make them feel better, he never hesitated. That was how I saw it.

I also knew that Suki and Brian's relationship never stood a chance. They both had problems which they couldn't solve. Brian talked about Anita's betrayal; Suki talked about Tara's death. They seemed more like mutual therapists than a loving couple.

Brian also told me that Suki had never lived at Cotchford Farm. When he bought the farm the intention was that Suki was going to live with him, but it never happened. Suki had visited Brian from time to time, but she'd never moved in.

'She's a city girl,' Brian said. 'She's not comfortable in the country.'

When I first visited Cotchford Farm, I soon realised that no woman had ever lived in the house. The only evidence of any female presence I found was a few items of clothing in one of the wardrobes.

'Suki told me to get rid of them,' Brian said. 'She doesn't want them any more.'

According to Brian, Suki had still been grieving for Tara when they started to date. Today, I find it easier to understand her. I've suffered the same form of grief, and I know how hard it is to move on.

The memories are always present. And they hurt.

CHAPTER THREE

THE LOVE

BRIAN

After our first meeting, I had to endure two unbearably long, painful days before Brian rang. I lolled about in the apartment staring at the telephone. I lifted the receiver countless times to make sure that it was connected. I thought incessantly about Brian, longed for him and had prepared myself for losing him and getting on with my life.

Then, at last, the phone rang!

We chatted for a while and he asked if it was OK to ring me again. That was typical of Brian. Always polite and anxious to please. He told me he was at Cotchford Farm, but would I consider having dinner in London with him the following weekend?

'Yes, of course,' I said. 'Give me a ring and tell me when you'll be here.'

Brian rang me several times that week to make sure I hadn't changed my mind about going out with him. I, on the other hand, tried not to appear too eager.

'Yes, just call me and tell me when it suits you,' I told him.

Brian seemed as nervous as me when he came to fetch me. He arrived in a taxi and had brought me a bouquet of flowers, which he held out for me and flashed me a warm smile. I thought it was both sweet and romantic.

I remember Brian's discreet outfit; a striped velvet jacket in grey and black and a turtle-neck sweater. I think he wanted to avoid attention. Later, I began to notice that Brian was always well dressed when we were going out somewhere.

He stood outside my door, a bit shy and embarrassed, but he tried to look nonchalant. Suddenly, I blushed and felt a bit shy and didn't know what to do or say. Brian cleared his throat.

'You look very pretty,' he said smiling.

'Thanks,' I replied.

Brian helped me into the taxi and told the driver where to go. After a while, Brian nudged up closer to me, but I wanted to keep him at a distance.

We didn't know each other, our relationship was new and I know that he'd been spoilt and always got the girl he wanted. I liked the idea of him making an effort to get me, even though my heart almost betrayed me. I wanted him so badly.

The taxi stopped in front of a restaurant, somewhere behind Harrods in Knightsbridge, and Brian held the door open for me and helped me out. The restaurant was small and the décor plain, but the food was excellent.

We continued to talk about our lives. Brian described how he had always wanted to be a musician and play his own music. He also had a desire to develop and learn to play many different instruments.

He didn't talk about the Stones, except in passing. I didn't reflect upon his reluctance then, although later I understood why he didn't want to talk about his work.

'Do you have a boyfriend?' he suddenly asked.

'Not one ... several,' I teased him.

Brian looked worried and I thought I should explain myself.

'I have friends who are boys,' I said. 'But I don't have a boyfriend.'

'I see,' Brian exclaimed.

He began to tell me about Cotchford Farm. When he talked about his house, his garden and his pride, the private lane, I was captivated by his enthusiasm.

'I have never liked a place as much as I like Cotchford Farm,' he said. 'You must come and see me sometime.'

'Maybe I will.'

'I'm restoring the house,' he continued. 'It's quite old and there's loads to do before it's finished.'

Brian described his ultra-modern kitchen with the beams and old stone floors. He talked about his music room and his bedroom, about his garden and what he was planning to sow in the spring, and he told me with pride that he had his very own swimming pool.

'I'm longing for the summer when I can mooch about in the garden and take a swim whenever I feel like it,' he said. 'Do you like to swim?'

I nodded.

'Then we'll swim together. We can sunbathe and swim ... all summer.'

'Mmm, that sounds really nice,' I said in a non-committal way, wishing secretly to cry out in sheer happiness.

He wanted to see me again!

*   *   *

Over the following weeks, Brian and I saw each other as often as we could. He was attracted to me, and seemed to want me as much as I wanted him. I could feel it in my heart.

Brian invited me out for dinners at small discreet restaurants in Knightsbridge or Chelsea. The restaurants had no names and the guests always brought their own wine. Brian preferred German wines, his favourite being Blue Nun.

Brian had good manners and was always a gentleman. He paid me compliments and brought me flowers, he held doors open for me and was courteous and polite. And he made me laugh.

I always tried to be unobtrusive, but he used to take my hand and introduce me to his acquaintances. He said that I was the one he wanted to be with and that he wasn't ashamed to show it.

Our first weeks together went by in a blur of romance and excitement and Brian continued to be romantic even after I had moved in with him. He was always waiting on me and paid me the utmost attention throughout the short time we had together.

When I think about Brian today, I always see him dressed up in a white suit and hat, with a flapping scarf around his neck. I'm convinced that he couldn't live without his multicoloured scarves, or his white suits.

I used to tease him and call him a 'snob-hippie'. He was so aware of every little detail and he always chose his clothes from his overflowing wardrobes with great care.

I didn't have the means to buy expensive clothes, but I knew what was trendy, and when I didn't make new outfits myself, I borrowed clothes from a girlfriend, who worked as a model.

One night, we were going out for dinner, and I was dressed in an almost transparent skirt, a leather jacket, jewellery and a pair of nice-looking shoes.

'Look who's attracting attention tonight!' Brian laughed. 'I'm sure everyone'll wonder who you are.'

'I suppose so, because they probably haven't got a clue who *you* are!' I teased him.

We were shown to a small, romantic booth in the restaurant,

and when I glanced at the other diners, I knew that they had recognised Brian. They looked at him and whispered to each other. Brian was used to being stared at and wasn't the slightest bit bothered by their curious looks — but I was. I felt awkward when people stared and whispered.

The waiter approached us and I quickly gave him my order. When I'd finished, I glanced at Brian.

'My cousin can't decide what he wants,' I said to the waiter. 'He's heartbroken, and we've come here to solve his problems. If you don't mind, we'd appreciate it if we were left in peace.'

The waiter looked sympathetic and recommended a couple of dishes to Brian, who played along, putting on an unhappy face. When the waiter had gone, Brian put his napkin over his face and laughed quietly. The waiter probably thought he was crying. I succeeded in maintaining a concerned look.

'What a little liar you are,' Brian said smiling, and I was quite proud of my inventiveness. It was a relief that nobody had to speculate on who I was. At least, it was for me.

'Do you find it hard to go out with me?' he asked. Without waiting for my answer, he continued, 'I'm used to all the attention, but I know it can be a pain in the arse from time to time. That's the price you have to pay when you're well known.

'In the beginning, I longed for this kind of attention. I didn't realise what it meant never to have any privacy. I felt a need to be somebody. I wanted to be famous and early on we loved every headline. It was important for us to be seen in the right or even the wrong places.

'But after a while, it all became too much for me. I know that the press has used me, but to be honest, I used them as well. I always saw to it they got the headlines they wanted, but that's all over now. I'm tired of making headlines.'

At the start of our relationship, I tried to act as if Brian and I were merely good friends. Brian didn't approve. And if we ran into someone who knew me, he also had to put up with being teased.

'Don't take Anna too seriously,' my friends would say. 'She has lots of admirers.'

Brian would become jumpy and I could see his concern.

'Don't mind them, they're only jealous,' I whispered, to calm him down.

We had a lot of fun and Brian appreciated my sense of humour. But he could be quite serious when the time came.

*   *   *

One evening, I sensed something in the air. We drove to one of our favourite restaurants and I remember ordering fillet of beef, vegetables and potatoes, Brian's favourite dish. But this evening, he didn't touch his food. I didn't either. Our legs intertwined under the table and, after a long silence, Brian looked me straight in the eye.

'I want more,' he said. 'Much more.'

We toyed with our food and looked at each other. The world ceased to exist — it was just us.

Brian had come to me of his own free will. I wanted him to take the first step. I wanted his feelings to be genuine. And that evening it felt as if my dream was coming true.

'I don't care what country you come from or what you've been doing before we met,' Brian said and took my hand. 'I want you.'

'When you get to know me better, you might not . . .' I said.

'Yes, I will. I've made up my mind. I want you and I hope that you want me. I want us to be together.

'You make me happy and I enjoy your company.'

I was choked with happiness and speechless. I suddenly felt really insecure. My dream had come true, but my self-confidence had evaporated. I was a nobody and Brian could have had whoever he wanted. Why did he want me?

'It's you I want. Nobody else,' he said softly.

'Please, take me home,' I murmured.

I needed to be alone to think about what he had said. I was in love, but at the same time I was frightened of deepening our relationship.

Brian didn't object and an hour later we were standing outside my house. He asked if he could come in.

'No,' I said.

'Why not? You haven't got a boyfriend stashed away in there, have you?' he asked, half-joking.

'No.'

His expression told me that my answer didn't completely convince him.

*   *   *

It felt like an age before I heard from Brian again. I was in love and the mere thought of him made my heart beat faster. I was unable to concentrate and I was torn between hope and despair. One minute I was walking on clouds, the next my restlessness made me feel sick. What if he'd never contact me again?

But he did. A couple of days later.

'Have you missed me?' a sweet voice asked when I answered the telephone. My heart leapt.

'Yes, a lot!' I almost shouted.

We chatted for a while and he promised to ring me in the next couple of days. I was overjoyed when I hung up. I danced around the apartment and my girlfriend didn't get a single word of sense out of me.

Brian rang me the next day and we decided to meet that evening.

It turned out to be an evening I would never forget.

CHAPTER FOUR

BRIAN

The car stopped in front of a small inn. It was dark and the trees stood out as silhouettes against the star-filled night sky. The softly-lit inn looked warm, inviting and romantic.

Brian stepped out and held the car door open for me. He took my hand and we walked towards the front door. I thought we were going to have dinner, but Brian went up to the landlord and booked a room for the night.

'Do you mind if we eat in our room?' Brian asked me. 'Is there something special you'd like to order?'

I couldn't speak. I don't know what I'd expected, but it wasn't this. I suddenly felt nervous.

When I'd dressed that evening I'd wondered about Brian's plans for the night. I wasn't in the mood to go to a restaurant and I didn't fancy going to a club. I wanted to be alone with him — so why did I hesitate?

Brian had smiled at me when I opened the front door to him. He was smartly dressed in a beige suit, his favourite matching hat and a loose scarf around his neck. He gave me a kiss and escorted me to the car he'd hired. The chauffeur nodded politely at me.

'Tonight, it's the lady's choice!' he said with a wink. 'I leave it to you to decide what we're doing.'

When the car had driven off, he leaned towards me and dropped his hat. He tossed it aside and gave me a kiss on the cheek.

'I've missed you,' he whispered.

He straightened his back and looked at me with a smile and my heart leapt. We drove aimlessly around London chatting about nothing in particularly. After half an hour, Brian asked me what I wanted to do.

I knew what I wanted, but I couldn't bring myself to say it — that I only wanted to make love to him. Brian read my mind and leaned towards the chauffeur, giving him brief directions. Then he sank down next to me and told me to tell him if I felt uncomfortable.

We drove further and further away from London and I started to feel anxious. What if we didn't get along? What if we had an argument?

In spite of my fears, I felt safe next to Brian with his hand in mine, and after a while I felt a sense of wellbeing warm my body. You have to give Brian a chance, I said to myself. If you are too scared to give in to your feelings, you'll regret it for the rest of your life. What have you got to lose? I asked myself. The answer was obvious. Nothing. Absolutely nothing. On the contrary, I had every chance of winning the man of my dreams.

But I was nervous and, now, standing in front of the landlord, I felt slightly embarrassed. We were not alone in the foyer and I was convinced that people had recognised Brian. What will they think of me? I asked myself. And then I couldn't help but wonder if Brian had brought women to this inn before.

The landlord hadn't moved a muscle when Brian had walked in and that reassured me a little. But I still felt self-conscious and Brian sensed my unease. He tried to make me feel a little more comfortable.

'Maybe we should go back,' I said in a low voice. 'You can always pick up another girl and bring her here.'

The words flew out before I could stop myself and I instantly regretted them. I couldn't avoid seeing that Brian was hurt.

'Brian, please, could I talk to you?' I said hurriedly.

He asked me what was wrong.

'Please, I need to talk to you alone,' I said.

I suddenly felt sick. My feelings ran high and I wanted to explain why I was worried, but I had trouble finding the words.

Brian took me outside. He put his arm round me and gave me a consoling smile.

'I think I can guess what's eating you,' he said. 'You're wondering if I always bring girls to hotels ... Am I right?'

I nodded.

'To be frank, I used to when we were on tour and stayed at different hotels. But I have never taken a girl to a hotel, neither in London nor outside London.

'Is that OK, Anna? It's really important that you believe me. If you'd prefer, we could go back to London or have a meal here first. I don't want to force you into something you don't want.'

I calmed down and told Brian that my only wish was to be with him. He gave me a kiss and a hug and we went back into the inn again.

We ordered salmon, caviar, avocado with shrimps, toast and white wine and then we went upstairs to our room.

Brian took my hand and looked into my eyes several times to be certain that I hadn't changed my mind. I reassured him that I hadn't.

When we reached the door, he swept me up into his arms and

carried me into the room. He went straight to the bed and carefully put me down.

'Are you sure you haven't changed your mind?' he asked again.

I couldn't speak, I just nodded and smiled. It was perfect, the romantic room with its thick, red carpet, the bed with its luxurious quilt covers, the soft lighting and Brian, of course. I felt as though I was living one of my fantasies, as I'd been dreaming about this moment seemingly for eternity — our first night together.

Brian closed the door and sat down next to me. He started to kiss and caress me and in a few minutes we couldn't hold back any longer and tore our clothes off. We made love twice before a girl arrived with a tray filled with our dinner order.

We had a glass of wine and a snack, and then I dozed off. I curled up with Brian, content and very happy.

When I woke, it was 2.00am. I stretched and Brian playfully tweaked my ear.

'I want to be close to you,' he whispered. 'Always.'

We caressed each other for a while and then decided to take a bath. We lay in the bath together and whispered softly to each other. Nothing else mattered. The most important thing was to be near him, to touch him and caress him.

Brian dried me off with a soft towel and carried me back to bed. We made love again, deeply and tenderly, and I knew that I would never give him up. He was the love of my life.

'You make me so happy and content,' he said. 'You're ... wonderful.'

I revelled in his words and intimacy and felt certain that I was as happy as I ever could hope to be. I wished that the night would never end.

Brian fetched two glasses of wine and the tray and placed it between us in the bed. It was the first time we had ever eaten in bed together, but it would not be the last — Brian loved that particular indulgence.

That night I also saw Brian's impulsive and fun-loving nature. Without saying a word, he suddenly jumped out of bed and collected a bath towel from the bathroom. He spread it on the floor and took the tray from the bed and placed it on the improvised rug.

'Welcome to our first picnic, Anna,' he said and pulled me down on to the towel. 'Remember, nothing is either good or bad until you've tried it.'

We ate and drank and Brian started to tell me about Morocco, the country which, according to him, had everything anyone could hope for. He talked about the fantastic light, the incredible blue of the sky, the culture, the people, the mystery, the sounds, the smells and, above all, the music. He was bewitched and his fascination was infectious.

He told me about his friend Brion Gysin, who lived in Morocco, and who had brought him to the master musicians of Jajouka where he had recorded the most fascinating music he had ever heard. He said that the tapes had inspired him to try to create a new kind of music. He wasn't sure how to do it yet, but he wanted me to listen to his tapes.

Brian was a gifted storyteller. When he described Morocco, I could see it in my mind and he made it sound as though nothing else could possibly live up to its magic. But he wasn't blind to the drawbacks in the country. He was aware of the injustice, the poverty, the pushers, the thieves and the prostitution.

'Anna,' he said in a serious voice, 'you have to come with me to Morocco. I want you to experience a new world and meet all those good people.'

That was typical of Brian. He always talked about the good things, the positive things. I would soon learn that Brian never spoke ill of people. I respected him for that. I seldom heard him run a person down. He always seemed to find an excuse for the bad behaviour of others.

*   *   *

It was a long and lovely night and we didn't get to sleep until almost dawn. Brian snuggled up behind me with his arms around me. Our legs were intertwined and we held each other's hands. It was the first time I'd slept beside him and it felt like a wonderful dream.

When I woke up the following day, Brian leaned over me and flashed his sunny smile, which I had already come to love. I returned it and pulled him down towards me, and kissed him. I wished that we could stay in that perfect room for the rest of our lives.

But I had to work in the afternoon and Brian had some errands to run in London. We had to get ready for the journey back.

While I took a shower and brushed my teeth — somehow, Brian had managed to conjure up some toothbrushes and toothpaste — breakfast was ordered. It was a typical English breakfast consisting of fruit juice, bacon, fried eggs, toast, marmalade, tea and two pints of rich milk!

I was content with a few slices of bread with marmalade and a glass of juice. Brian tried to persuade me to drink some milk, but I refused. He delivered a long (and boring) lecture and told me that there were numerous wholesome vitamins and minerals in milk, but I didn't let him have his way. I would drink milk in Sweden, but I didn't trust English milk, and I found it too rich.

While we were having breakfast, Brian suddenly stopped eating and looked at me.

'Anna, I want you to make me a promise. I want you always to make my bacon crispy.'

I think it was love.

Shortly before we left the inn, Brian sneaked up behind me and put his arms around me.

'I know that you and I belong together,' he said.

I shivered with pleasure, but I wasn't sure if I could trust him or not.

I don't know where our chauffeur had slept that night and I didn't ask. I presumed that he and Brian had come to some kind of agreement — or maybe it was a different chauffeur! I'm not sure. I only had eyes for the new man in my life.

On the way back to London, I leaned against Brian. He kissed and hugged me from time to time, and we just chatted idly. We were both tired and lost in our own thoughts.

When we approached London, I started to feel anxious. Brian felt my tension and gave me a puzzled look.

'What's the matter? Is something worrying you?'

I didn't know how to explain my unease.

'There's no need to worry about anything!' he said and hugged me.

I wasn't as sure as he seemed to be. I couldn't help wondering whether I was a one-night-stand or if he really was serious about me. I wasn't a virgin. Remember, this was in the Sixties when 'free love' was in plentiful supply and, of course, I had had my share of other men.

But this was something else. For the first time in my life, I was emotionally involved with a man. I had been in love with Brian for five years. I didn't want to end up as a footnote in his life.

The car stopped in front of my house. A feeling of emptiness washed over me. I didn't want to leave him. What if I never saw him again?

Brian stepped out and held out his hand to me. He gave me a hug and a kiss.

'I'll ring you,' he whispered.

Three familiar words. Three misused words. The three most

CHAPTER FIVE

THE FARM

BRIAN

Brian was right. I didn't have to worry. After our first night together, our telephone conversations became more frequent, starting with a call Brian made to me just hours after our drive back from the inn. So he did keep his promise.

'Do you still like me a little?' he asked.

'Yes ... a wee bit,' I answered.

I was afraid that I would scare him away if I seemed overly worried. Sometimes, it's the wrong strategy to choose. In Brian's case, it definitely was.

'Do you miss me?' he continued.

'A wee bit,' I said again, in a nonchalant tone.

Weeks later, Brian told me that he was overjoyed when I admitted that I missed him. He'd forgotten that I had said 'a little'. I soon realised that Brian craved affection and that he needed to know that he was desirable and loved.

I had to learn always to be honest with him about my feelings.

I never had to pretend with him and I soon found it to be a great relief.

*   *   *

The next time Brian showed up on my doorstep, he had hired a limousine. On the seat in the back of the car I found a bouquet of red roses, which he gave me with a smile.

'I bought these for you, love,' he said and kissed me. 'How are you? All right?'

'Yes, I am now that you're here,' I answered and kissed him back. Brian told me that he wasn't in the mood to have dinner and he asked me if I was hungry. I wasn't.

So Brian asked the chauffeur to drive us to a small park outside London. I'm not sure where it was; I was too absorbed with Brian to notice the direction, but I remember a beautiful church next to the park.

We strolled around, hand in hand, and were happy just being together. I still found it hard to believe that he had chosen me out of hundreds of girls. Did he really want *me*?

Yes, my heart sang.

Brian was romantic and considerate and the night ended in the back of the limousine where we made passionate love. Brian kept my knickers as a trophy. It was a habit he'd repeat every time we met. He always took something from me to be certain that we'd meet again.

*   *   *

A couple of weeks later, Brian invited me to Cotchford Farm. It was early spring 1969. I was beside myself with joy.

Brian told me to take a taxi and on the journey down to Cotchford Farm I tried to remember what Brian had told me about his country home.

I knew he had fallen in love with the house and the garden at first sight and that he was overjoyed to live in 'Pooh's' house. He had told me about the statuettes in the garden; Winnie the Pooh, Piglet, Eeyore and all the other characters from the books. He also mentioned that he was thinking of putting the statuette of Christopher Robin in the kitchen to remind him that two of the world's most popular stories had been written in the beautiful farmhouse. It was magical to him, it was history at its best. And Brian loved everything that had a history.

Brian waxed lyrical when he talked about his house, the plants and the vegetable garden, his swimming pool, his very own lane, and the small stream that flowed alongside the garden. He was deeply attached to his home. Not only because Winnie the Pooh's creator, AA Milne, had lived there, but also because he thought that Cotchford Farm was the most beautiful place in the world. I was looking forward to seeing Brian's beloved home, but at the same time I felt a little tense.

When the taxi turned off the narrow gravel road and drove down the private lane I was overwhelmed by the beauty of the landscape. The lane was lined on both sides with thick foliage, reminding me of fairytale princes and princesses, and I knew that at the end of the lane my own prince would be waiting for me to enter his castle.

The car eventually stopped in front of a lovely old stone house. It was beautifully still, and the only thing breaking the silence was the sound of a piano, which floated towards me from the house. At first I thought Brian was playing, but later discovered that it had been a Liberace album.

It seemed that Brian was as tense as me, or maybe he wanted to impress me, by playing the music so loudly.

The front door opened before I'd stepped out of the car. Brian came out, accompanied by his dogs, a black Afghan and a black-

and-white cocker spaniel.

Brian wore a pair of light-coloured trousers and a white jacket. He had a felt hat on his head — and an air-gun casually resting on his shoulder!

Brian was the living image of Christopher Robin and his beloved pop gun.

He flung his arms round my neck and gave me a kiss.

'I've been longing for you,' he whispered.

Later, he told me that he had felt nervous about me not liking his house. He was afraid that it was not good enough. He needn't have worried. I came to love the house and its surroundings almost as much as I loved him.

Brian paid the taxi driver, took my suitcase and showed me into the house. The dogs ran happily around our feet and barked to get our attention, but we were too busy hugging and kissing.

When we got into the house, Brian put down my suitcase and the air-gun and closed the door. Then he turned, pulled me into his arms and started kissing me.

We were in love and we could not resist each other. We ended up making love on the stone floor in the small hall beside an armchair. It was quite uncomfortable, but wonderful at the same time, and I felt all my tension disappear.

When we got up, we straightened our clothing and laughed. Brian picked up his air-gun and dragged me out into the garden. He fired a couple of shots into the air and smiled happily at me.

'Can I try?' I asked and Brian showed me how to hold the gun to avoid being hurt.

I fired a shot and I was almost thrown backwards. I decided that I wasn't keen on air-guns.

Brian took me by the hand and we walked through the garden with the dogs. I asked their names and Brian told me that the Afghan was called Luther and that the cocker spaniel's was Emily.

Brian showed me the statuettes he had been telling me about

and the beautiful sundial with its engravings of Christopher Robin, Winnie the Pooh and all the other characters from the stories.

'I've been told that the original manuscripts for the books are hidden in the sundial's foundations,' Brian told me proudly.

We strolled on through the rose garden and up to the terraced lawns above the pool and I could almost feel the presence of Christopher Robin and his friends when I surveyed the garden. It was as if we were travelling back in time to our childhoods and I clearly understood why Brian found Cotchford Farm to be a heaven on earth.

In the garden, below the swimming pool, there was a little path where the bushes formed an arbour. Brian pulled me into that green paradise and we made love again. The secluded arbour became our love nest, a place to be alone with our love.

'I want you to be mine for ever,' Brian whispered, and we sealed our vows with a kiss. Neither of us could possibly have anticipated the cruel fate that was awaiting us.

I kept my promise and became his for ever, but not in the way he had wished for.

*   *   *

The three-storey farmhouse, or to be more exact, the three small houses which had been knocked together, was old and charming. Brian had tried to renovate and preserve the house as it used to be, but I didn't find the interior décor particularly tasteful. On the contrary, I noticed that there was a coldness about it, and I felt that it was lacking a woman's care and presence. It was evident that there had been quite a number of advisers — and that they had probably disagreed!

The old adage 'Too many cooks spoil the broth' is an apt description of the otherwise lovely house. At least, that was my personal opinion.

On entering through the front door you came into a small hall where there was also a cloakroom. To the right was a hallway which led to the staircase, Brian's favourite room — the music room — and a room where Brian kept his tapes. To the left was the dining room and the kitchen.

Brian had retained the old and worn flagstone floors. The smooth hollows in the flags were evidence of the many thousands of feet which must have brushed the floor over the centuries.

The music room was Brian's pride and joy and the most beautiful room in the house. It was situated in an extension to the house with its windows facing the driveway and the garden. There was also a door which led on to the garden.

You had to go down a couple of steps to enter the lovely room, and to the right of the stairs there was a large platform, almost like a small stage. Brian was especially fond of the flagstones covering the structure. They were ancient and faded and Brian had instructed the builders to treat the beautiful stones with care.

In the middle of the room was a huge fireplace, which I could easily stand in. To the left of the fireplace, Brian had his piano and several other instruments, and to the right there was a TV set. The only furniture in the room were a couple of easy chairs and a table.

Across the hallway, Brian had his so-called tape room. He kept all his recordings and even his albums in there. He always recorded the sessions he had with his friends, and among his tapes there were recordings from Jajouka, his session with John Lennon, who came down to visit us, as well as recordings with Alexis Korner, John Mayall and other musicians.

On the left side of the entrance you entered the dining room, which went right through the house with windows looking on to the driveway and windows and a door with leaded panes overlooking the garden. When the light slanted through the glass panes it lent the room a poetic feel and I always enjoyed sitting around the big wooden table, where we both entertained our guests and watched TV.

Along the right wall there was a lovely, antique sideboard with a shelf, where Brian kept the china plates. You could tell that Brian had no particular interest in china. He had just bought the necessary plates and bowls without caring too much about what they looked like. He thought he had time on his side, and could worry about all that in the future.

To reach the rectangular kitchen, which also ran from the front to the back of the house, you first had to go through the dining room. On the left, a couple of stairs up, in the other extension of the house, was the kitchen table and a couple of refrigerators and freezers.

Brian was especially proud of the pine kitchen table, which had been made from what he called a Scandinavian design. He was also proud of the beams in the ceiling which he had had the builder put up.

The kitchen sink faced the garden, and along the walls were, to the right, the stove and the grill, and to the left was a long bench. At one end of this was another fridge and a door with a large dog-flap leading to the garden. We seldom used the back door, apart from when I hung my underwear up on the laundry line, which was this end of the house.

I was spoilt when it came to cleaning clothes. Brian and I always sent our clothes, sheets and towels to the laundry every Wednesday and we got them back two days later. It was quite a luxury, but I soon discovered that there were always some small items missing. A sock, a pair of briefs or underpants, and that was why I preferred to wash my underwear by hand.

Next to the tape room was the staircase to the upper floors. The master bedroom was on the first floor and you reached it by walking to the far end of a hallway and up a small staircase. The bedroom went straight through the house with windows facing both the front and the garden. It was spacious and bright, but the décor was uninspiring. The walls were beige, as well as the curtains and the carpet. The dominant piece of furniture in the bedroom was a double mattress which lay on the floor and a bedside table on Brian's side of the bed, which faced the garden. The door was on my side of the bed and between the bed and the door we had the record-player. Above the bed hung a Gobelin tapestry, probably from Morocco.

There were a lot of rumours after Brian's death. Among other things, it was said that one of the builders had insisted that Brian kept a bundle of bank notes on his bedside table and that he used to pull notes out of the stack when the workmen asked for money to buy building materials.

I never saw a bundle of bank notes. All the invoices were sent straight to the Stones' accountant at the office in London. Brian never even saw them.

In front of the bed, along the bathroom wall, Brian had installed mirrored doors on the old wardrobes. On the left hand side of the wardrobes was the door to the huge bathroom. It was decorated in bright yellow on the walls, and had a black washbasin, toilet and bathtub. The wall above the bathtub was covered with glazed tiles.

Brian wasn't interested in the basics of colour. The only things he cared about were his precious wardrobes. In the bathroom he had wardrobes along one of the short walls and a couple more on a side wall. To this day, I have never seen, so many wardrobes in one place. And they were all overflowing with clothes and shoes.

Next to the master bedroom, down the small staircase, was the green bathroom and the green guest room which both faced the garden.

On the left of the staircase there was a small hallway and another smaller bedroom. Brian always referred to it as the nursery. Continuing along from the nursery there was a door to the staircase which led to the top floor and a big beautiful bedroom and yet another small room. Brian was convinced that these two rooms were once occupied by Christopher Robin.

To complete the tour, there were a further two small bedrooms, a bathroom and another large bedroom. Brian used the top floor as a store.

The house itself was wonderful but almost from the day I moved in, I was itching to change the interior décor. I was pleased that Brian had preserved a lot of the old characteristics of the house. But I didn't really think much of the way he combined original antiques with his odd souvenirs from Morocco. They seemed to me to be generally disgusting things in glaring colours and lots of brassware, and I thought the house was in dire need of a female touch.

*   *   *

In Sweden, we always enjoy sitting in the kitchen, a more informal setting than the dining room, and I instantly liked Brian's kitchen, perhaps because the pine table made me feel at home.

The first evening I spent at Cotchford Farm, Brian and I sat opposite each other at the kitchen table and talked about our childhood memories and our families, our youth and our dreams.

I always felt wonderfully at ease talking with Brian, and the nerves he'd suffered when I first arrived were soon forgotten. Eventually, I understood that Brian's self-confidence was skin-deep and that he really was quite shy and insecure. To my great delight, he was nothing like the tough boy I had read about in the papers.

Full of sadness, he told me about his sister Pamela, who had died of leukaemia when she was just a little girl. He told me that his mother, Louise, had unwittingly shut him out when he needed her love the most. She grieved for the loss of her daughter and was unable to understand his needs.

'Instead of giving me a hug and trying to understand and comfort me when I was being difficult, she pushed me away,' Brian said sadly. 'I felt rejected and unloved and I still don't know what she really thinks of me.'

When Brian started to talk about his father, Lewis, the light came back into his eyes.

'My father was always there for me,' Brian said with a smile. 'I love him deeply and I'm sad if I've disappointed him with my choice of career. I know that he wanted me to graduate, but I always wanted to be a musician, right from the time when I first heard Mum play the piano.

'I don't regret a thing, though, and I hope one day Dad will understand me.'

I told Brian about my parents and their disappointment when I went to London instead of continuing with my education. Like me, Brian came from the middle-classes and our upbringings were generally conservative. We were both rebels, albeit in different ways, and we understood each other.

Right from the start, Brian and I felt that we had a lot in common. We had chosen to lead our lives the way we wanted, and not according to our parents' expectations. But, funnily enough, we soon discovered that we were beginning to understand our parents and their bourgeois lives and that we were even starting to adopt their values and accept the choices they had made for themselves.

We talked about my situation and Brian repeated that he

would rather lock his daughter up than allow her to settle in a foreign country before she was 25.

'And that's that!' he exclaimed, putting his foot down.

I couldn't help laughing.

'What about you?' I teased. 'I thought you said you moved out when you were only 16?'

'That was different,' Brian said. 'It wasn't my choice. I'd made a girl pregnant and I had to scarper to avoid a scandal.'

He told me that he was homesick throughout his time in Germany and he'd thought his parents had let him down when he needed them most. He was young and naïve and said that neither he nor the girl knew better. He'd been living in a slum district in Germany without money and friends. He felt that he'd been frozen out by his family and didn't know how to set things right again.

'I started to revolt at an early age,' he went on. 'I saw that there was a lot wrong with our society and I enjoyed provoking people to see how far I could bend the rules, which I thought were just too old-fashioned.

'When I was young, I thought my parents led a sheltered, boring life, but I suppose I can appreciate their lifestyle a bit more now I've met you.

'I've seen so much misery and been involved in too much crap. Most of it caused by drugs and all the hangers-on. I used to think of them as friends.'

Brian told me he now wanted a whole new life; a family to work for. He was no longer content just working for fame and fortune.

'My most fervent wish is to be reunited with my sons, Julian and Mark,' he said. 'I sometimes feel really guilty and I hope I'll be able to make it up to them soon. I know I've not been a great father and I hope they'll give me a second chance to get to know them better.

'Hey — wouldn't it be great if they could visit us during their school holidays?' he said with a grin. 'I think they'd like it here ... don't you?'

'Mmm . . .' I agreed.

'I don't know ... maybe men don't have the same feelings as women,' he went on. 'But I really love my sons and I hope I'll be able to prove it to them some day. I've missed them so much over the last few years, and I want to make it up to them, the best way I can.'

Brian told me that he'd been prepared to be a loving father to Julian when he was born, that he felt proud of him and wanted to accept his responsibility. But it hadn't worked out. He'd had too many irons in the fire at the time and the music came before anything else in those days.

Later, when Mark was born, he was still naïve and in retrospect he felt that he'd had neither the time nor the knowledge to take care of his sons the way he wanted.

During our conversations, the subject constantly returned to Brian's sons and his feelings of guilt. Maybe that was why he hoped that our first child would be a girl.

*   *   *

Brian and I shared a bottle of wine while we were talking. We'd put candles on the table and it was both cosy and romantic.

'Anna, wait there a mo', will you?' Brian suddenly said. 'I've got a surprise for us. I just feel like it.'

He stood up and disappeared, but only for a few moments. He returned with his guitar.

He sat down, looked at me with a beautiful smile and started to play. After a while, he began to sing.

'Time ... time ... time is on my side ...' He stopped for a second, and said, 'No, hang on ...' Then he sang again, 'Time ... time ... time is on *our* side. Yes, it is . . .'

He winked at me when he changed 'my' to 'our'. When the last note had sounded, he remained quite still for a moment.

'Usually I hate to sing,' he said at last. 'In fact, I've only done it once before at a recording session. But tonight I just felt like it.'

Brian wasn't exactly an opera singer, but with a little bit of practice he could have been quite good.

'I haven't touched my guitar for ages,' he said. 'And I've never really felt like singing. You must have inspired me ... you make me feel I can do anything!'

I couldn't take my eyes off him. He looked like an angel with his long, blond hair and his enchanting smile. It was such a wonderful moment.

Later that evening, Brian rang his father and told him about me and said that he was happy that we'd met. He also said that he missed his parents and asked if they would like to come and see him soon.

I don't know if it was me who'd made him think of his family and ring his father. I'd tried to explain that it must be hard for a mother to see one of her beloved children gradually waste away. I talked about the grief, the anger and the powerlessness she must have felt and which had made her forget about almost everything else, such as Brian and his little sister Barbara, and the sorrow and hurt they must have felt as well.

I think Brian heard me and maybe it helped him to understand his mother a little better.

The night was long and wonderful, and the following day we didn't get out of bed until almost 1.00pm. I was blissfully happy. I felt like I'd come home. It felt natural sleeping beside him with his arms around me.

'Anna, you make me feel confident, loved and important,' Brian said, 'and I want you to know that you're the most important person in my life. Never forget that. I don't understand why I always have to remind you that you're the best thing that's ever happened to me!'

Brian was always ready to tell me how much he loved me, for being natural and unaffected as he put it.

On Saturday afternoon, Brian told me that he was going to prove just how serious he was about me. He picked up the phone and called a taxi.

'Come on,' he said. 'We're going down to the village.'

We went down to a local pub, the Hay Waggon Inn in Hartfield, and Brian introduced me to everyone.

'This is my girlfriend, Anna,' he said. 'She's from Sweden and she's here to stay.'

I was surprised and a bit embarrassed, but at the same time I thought that it was sweet of him to introduce me publicly. I didn't realise the extent of his announcement until we were back at the farmhouse.

'Now they can ring the papers and reveal that I've got a new girlfriend,' Brian said.

Later that evening, we were sitting in the garden when Brian suddenly stopped talking. A moment later, he turned towards me and said, 'I want you to come and live with me.'

I stared at him, unable to decide whether I should take him seriously. But he insisted.

The following night, neither of us could sleep. We only had one day left. And Brian tried to convince me to move in with him as soon as possible.

'Come on ... we're really suited for each other,' he insisted. 'Please, Anna, come and live with me.'

I had never lived with a man before and Brian and I had only known each other for a short time. I felt it was too soon. I needed some thinking time.

The next morning, Brian went down to the kitchen and made me breakfast. Tea, toast ... and a big glass of milk! He never gave up. He was really stubborn about the milk. Every morning he'd try to make me drink the full-fat milk, which he himself couldn't live without.

Brian was considerate, tender and sweet all day. He didn't want me to go back to London, but we both knew that he had to come to terms with his old life and break up with Suki before we could start a life together. Brian hadn't told Suki about me, and she didn't even know that I existed.

'I promise I'll talk to Suki this coming week,' Brian said. 'And as soon as I've done it, I want you to come to live with me ... please?'

I laughed and kissed him. He was the most persistent man I'd ever met — and I loved him for it.

In the afternoon, Brian decided to put me to the test. He came out into the garden where I was sunbathing and wanted me to follow him. He escorted me to the kitchen, opened the fridge and took out a big steak, potatoes and vegetables.

'I thought we could have this for dinner,' he said. 'Can you cook it?'

'Yes, of course,' I said and crossed my fingers.

I'd never cooked anything in my life, but I was sure that it would work out, one way or another. My grandfather launched the first smokehouse in Stockholm and my uncles are still in the business. My mother is an excellent cook, but I was never interested in cooking when I was growing up and, as a consequence, I didn't know anything about food preparation.

I wished that I'd inherited her skills and bitterly regretted my lack of interest.

Brian was no help. His culinary skills were even worse than mine. The only thing he could make was a sandwich — lettuce, tomatoes, cucumber and then something slapped in the middle!

Brian left the kitchen whistling cheerfully, and went out into the garden with Luther and Emily. There I was, alone with a big, raw lump of meat and some vegetables.

I tried to remember what my mother used to do, but I could only remember the tiniest details. So I spiced the meat and cleaned the potatoes and the vegetables.

Then I put the lot on a baking sheet and pushed it into a hot oven, and joined Brian in the garden.

We sat down and enjoyed the stillness of the beautiful spring day. Time passed and I suddenly smelt something burning. At first, we thought that the kitchen was on fire and we rushed in to see what had happened. We then realised that the black smoke was pouring out of the oven.

Well, the meat was perfectly roasted, but the rest of the meal was a little over-done — carbonised, in fact.

Brian collapsed in a fit of giggles at my culinary expertise. But he was hungry and tucked bravely into the steak.

My failure as a cook made me realise that I had to pick up some tips, and when I eventually moved in with Brian I often sneaked down to Mrs Hallett, who regularly helped around the house with the housework, and asked her advice. Sometimes, I even rang my mother.

A few weeks later, Brian said that he'd wanted to test me. He didn't expect me to be able to cook. He was sure that I'd refuse and suggest that we went out to a restaurant instead.

*   *   *

The day I first visited Cotchford Farm, I made a new friend — Emily, the beautiful cocker spaniel. She happily followed me around and slept at my feet at night. Brian couldn't understand why she was so attracted to me and became a bit jealous.

He told me that he'd had no intention of getting a dog when he bought Emily. It had just happened. He and Suki had been strolling around Harrods and had ended up in the pet department. A black-and-white puppy had been sitting in one of the cages and looked imploringly at him with her sad eyes. Suki owned a golden-brown cocker spaniel, Matilda, and Brian was under the impression that all cocker spaniels were the same colour. He'd never seen a black-and-white cocker spaniel before and, surprised, he stopped to have a closer look at her.

He looked at the puppy for a while and then continued with his shopping. But the puppy's eyes had stayed vividly in his mind and after a while he returned to the pet department.

The cocker spaniel was sitting in exactly the same place as before and she didn't take her eyes off him. He picked her up and she joyfully licked and kissed him. Brian didn't have the heart to put her back in the cage. He bought her and called her Emily.

'She was the ugliest puppy of the lot,' he said. 'But I didn't have the heart to leave her there. She'd probably have grown old and even uglier before someone had taken pity on her.'

But Emily wasn't ugly. She was a beautiful young lady and I'm not sure that it was Brian's choice to buy her. I think Emily had chosen him as her master. Maybe she felt that he needed her.

Luther wasn't a planned purchase either. The black Afghan was two years old when he found Brian. A breeder in the neighbourhood had had him returned from his original buyers and she didn't know what to do with him. Eventually, she asked Brian if he would consider taking care of the dog.

One of Brian's weaknesses was his inability to say 'no', and Luther eventually moved in with Brian and Emily at Cotchford Farm.

Luther was like a big, shaggy baby. He was constantly running away to explore his surroundings. Brian and I would spend hours looking for him. Quite often one of our neighbours would arrive on our doorstep with a happy Luther in tow, and then proceed to give us an earful about his lack of training.

Luther was a happy and carefree dog, who lived according to his own rules. He was hopeless when it came to training and in some way I think he reminded Brian of himself, or perhaps the way he was as a teenager. Maybe that was one of the reasons why Brian loved him.

I often teased Brian when his voice became husky from calling Luther.

'Maybe this will help you to understand your parents. It's not easy when you've either got teenagers or pets with their own ideas!'

Luther was not a lap dog like Emily. He was independent and by his own choice lived in the kitchen. He was devoted to Brian in an unconventional way, but I never doubted that he loved his master. I often saw them side by side, except, of course, when Luther ran off!

Emily and Luther were not the only dogs I met on my first weekend at Cotchford Farm. Suki had left Matilda in Brian's care and the sight of her in the house confirmed that Suki was still very much on the scene.

*   *   *

When I returned to London on the Sunday night I was exhilarated. I started missing Brian on my way home, but I didn't think that he would miss me as much as I missed him. I was wrong.

I hadn't even had time to close the door to the apartment before the phone rang. It was Brian. He told me his missed me and longed for me. The following day, he rang seven times, only to say that he missed me, longed for me and loved me. He continued to ring me every day until Friday morning.

'A car will pick you up after lunch,' Brian said when I answered the telephone. 'Pack all your stuff and come live with me. I've talked it over with Suki. You needn't worry about a thing. She understands.'

I packed one suitcase, as I still wasn't convinced that he was serious about me moving in with him, and I rang the shopkeeper I was working for. It was just casual work and I knew she wouldn't mind me leaving at short notice. I explained that I'd met a wonderful man and that I was moving in with him.

I decided not to tell her his name or his occupation, for fear of tempting fate.

It was too soon.

CHAPTER SIX

THE
HAPPINESS

BRIAN

I moved in with Brian on a Friday afternoon in early May. In London, the sky was bright blue and the brilliant sunshine made me hopeful about the future. I was walking on air, my heart singing with joy and longing to be reunited with my fairytale prince.

At exactly 2.00pm, a taxi drove up and my journey began. By that time, I'd paced up and down my friend's apartment for hours waiting for the car to arrive.

'Are you just staying for the weekend?' Brian asked with a frown when he noticed my lone suitcase. 'Are you going back to London?'

I told him I hadn't had the time to pack all my things. I didn't want to hurt his feelings by telling him that I was still a little unsure about his invitation.

Brian accepted my explanation and carried my suitcase into the house.

*   *   *

My first weekend in my new home was wonderful. Brian and I enjoyed each other's company, as only a couple in love can do. We hugged and we joked and couldn't get enough of each other. Everything was surrounded by a romantic aura and I was happier than I had ever been before.

We skinny-dipped in the heated pool, strolled in the garden and played with the dogs. Matilda was still there, but Brian told me that Suki had promised to come for her as soon as she could find the time.

I tried to make friends with Matilda, but she wasn't interested. She was a one-man, or in this case, a one-woman dog. She kept her distance and trotted along by herself.

Since neither Brian nor I wanted to leave the farm, I had to cook. At least I had learned from my earlier mistake and I cooked some meat, potatoes and vegetables separately. The food was edible. Success!

But eating was not our biggest concern. We were alone and we were together, and that was the most important thing to us.

When the working week began, our idyllic peace was shattered. A terrible noise woke me up with a start. The workmen had arrived!

I looked over to the window facing the driveway and came face-to-face with a man on a ladder staring at me. Brian had told me that they would be working on the front of the house, but I had no idea what they would be doing — and neither did he.

I didn't know which way to turn. I was naked and didn't dare to leave the bed. After a while, he climbed down and I hurried to the bathroom. I was annoyed that our tranquility had been interrupted in such a noisy way.

In the bathroom I found a dressing gown and returned to the

bedroom. Brian was still sleeping soundly. After eight months, he had apparently got used to the awful noise.

I picked up my clothes and went back to the bathroom to get dressed and put on my make-up. After a while, Brian woke up and flashed me a radiant smile, and I threw myself into his arms.

Brian got up and dressed and together we went down to the kitchen where he introduced me to Mrs Hallett. I took to her at once. She was friendly, sweet and confident.

That morning, we had our breakfast in the kitchen while Brian chatted with Mrs Hallett about the day's housework.

Mrs Hallett, who was born on Cotchford Farm, helped with cleaning the house and took on various other household duties as and when they cropped up. But she never cooked. That was to become my responsibility.

Brian explained that in future I would also prepare his breakfast.

'She has promised me crispy bacon ... ,' he said and smiled at me. 'Exactly how I like it.'

I could tell that Mrs Hallett felt a bit slighted. She obviously loved looking after Brian. But she gave in to his wish and from then on I became the cook of the house, whether I wanted to or not.

A while later, when we sat in the garden enjoying the sunshine, Brian told me about Mrs Hallett and his gardener, Mick Martin. He said that he didn't know how to take care of a house or garden and because of that he had made it a condition to the broker that Mrs Hallett and Mick Martin should continue to work at Cotchford Farm if he bought the house. They accepted and Brian was delighted with the arrangement.

After that Monday, our mornings became a special time of day for us. We usually woke up around 9.00am when the workmen arrived and, thinking back, the one thing I miss the most is Brian's radiant smile. Each morning when he woke up, he looked at me and smiled this wonderfully happy smile, which I will never forget.

We usually stayed on in bed and cuddled for a while before I went downstairs, with Emily following close by, to prepare Brian's breakfast and have a cup of tea with Mrs Hallett, if she could find the time.

First, I'd let Emily out into the garden and then go to the kitchen and chat with Mrs Hallett. She was very sweet and thoughtful and gradually became almost a mother to me. I still remember the delight I felt soon after my arrival at the farm, when I was on my way into the kitchen. Mrs Hallett was talking to Mick who occasionally dropped in for a cup of coffee.

She told the gardener that Mr Jones, as she always called Brian, had met a nice girl from Sweden.

'I do hope that Anna stays, for the sake of Mr Jones,' I heard her say. My heart sang.

I know that Brian was extremely fond of Mrs Hallett and appreciated her sensitivity. She took great care of the house and she always made sure that the milkman delivered fresh milk every day. Brian was more like a baby calf than a human sometimes, and I'm quite sure that he drank at least five pints of milk a day, seldom bothering to fetch a glass. Usually he just opened the fridge and drank straight from the bottle.

Brian appreciated everything Mrs Hallett did for us. Only on one occasion did I ever see him a bit unhappy because of her.

One morning when I came down to the kitchen, Mrs Hallett said that she wanted to show me something.

'I have a surprise for Mr Jones,' she said and smiled excitedly. 'Please, come with me!'

She took me to the music room, down the stairs, and pointed at Brian's pride and joy, the platform. The old flagstones were shining like new!

'It took me a while because I had to polish every one of them by hand,' Mrs Hallett said proudly. 'It looks nice, don't you think? I hope Mr Jones will be pleased.'

I kept a straight face. 'I am *sure* he will,' I said. 'They look very nice.'

I knew that Brian loved his old, faded flagstones and I felt I should warn him. Mrs Hallett meant well and I knew she'd polished them to make Brian happy.

When Mrs Hallett went back to the kitchen, I rushed up the stairs. Brian was awake and I told him about the surprise.

Brian's expression went from panic-stricken to desperate to resigned. And then he started to laugh.

'She's a love,' he said. 'I'll probably hate it, but I can't tell her off. I know she did it to please me.'

Brian was like a sunbeam in the mornings. He never suffered from a bad mood. Not even this incident could destroy his good spirits and when he went down to the kitchen he thanked Mrs Hallett for making the stones look so beautiful.

That was the Brian I knew and had come to love. He could forgive almost anything.

Before I started to prepare his breakfast, I usually had a cup of tea and a slice of Swedish crispbread with Cheddar cheese. I encouraged Brian to eat crispbread and he soon wanted a slice with cheese every morning.

In addition to that, Brian's breakfast consisted of tea, a glass of juice, toast, fried egg, which should only be fried for a short time on each side because he liked the yolk runny, and crispy bacon. I put everything on a plate along with fresh tomatoes from the garden. And last, but not least, a bottle of milk!

Sometimes I took a shower before I went down to the kitchen and then, occasionally, Brian would pop his head into the bathroom and ask if I wanted him to make breakfast. I thought he was cute and felt spoilt when I returned to the bed and waited for him to serve up.

When Brian had finished his breakfast, I'd lie down beside him for a while. Some mornings we made love, but with the workmen outside, it never felt too comfortable. And Emily looked miserable when she was relegated to the floor and had to listen to music.

Music was an essential part of our life. We fell asleep listening to music and we woke up to it.

After we relaxed for a while, or made love, we used to get ready for the day ahead. Sometimes we took a bath together and I loved to wash Brian's hair. He liked me to cut it and while I tried to do that he invented a new position. He sat down on the toilet seat and pulled me down over him.

'I want to be inside you and make it nice for you while you cut my hair,' he said teasingly.

Of course, I couldn't concentrate on the haircut and soon we ended up in bed where we made wild and uninhibited love. We were deeply in love and very attracted to each other.

Brian was a wonderful lover. He was tender, considerate and very inventive. He never ceased to surprise me.

After the bath, or the love-making, we got dressed and I put mascara on my eyelashes in front of the mirrored doors in the bedroom and it was soon covered with black spots. Brian once asked me why I didn't use the bathroom mirror.

'If I did, you couldn't look at me,' I teased him.

Brian laughed and the subject never came up again.

Brian was almost never annoyed or angry, but he had a faculty for making even the smallest of problems seem huge. He could, for example, decide to move a bush in the garden and then a long discussion would follow about where it should be planted instead. It could go on for hours and eventually I'd get tired of the whole thing and tell him to plant the bloody bush wherever he wanted!

Brian constantly sought for peace in his soul, but his

insecurity made it difficult. I think that was one of the reasons he wanted to discuss everything with me. It was vital for him to hear my opinion, no matter how trivial it might be. He would not cease until we'd made a mutual decision which satisfied us both.

Right from the start, Brian always said 'we' instead of 'I'. It was important to him that we were a 'we'. Having never lived with a man before, I wasn't used to discussing every little detail or thinking of someone else when I made a decision. But it was important to Brian that we agreed everything, whatever it was.

The more I got to know him, the more I appreciated Brian's consideration. We had a spiritual affinity and my love for him deepened every day. And he spoilt me with his love and care. Not a day passed without Brian telling me he loved me, but he wasn't sure about my feelings for him and, at the start of our relationship, he was always afraid that I might leave him.

I, however, felt safe and secure right from the word go and such a thought never occurred to me. But Brian didn't know that. He needed to be close to me and have constant reassurance that I really loved him.

'Anna, it is just us, isn't it?' he used to say. 'Tell me you don't love anyone else. You want to live here, don't you? You do want to stay with me?'

Occasionally, it could take hours to convince him that I loved him and enjoyed our quiet life in the country. I felt a tremendous feeling of kinship when we finally started to laugh. We belonged together. There was never a doubt in my mind.

*　　　　*　　　　*

Brian went down to the kitchen every morning to have a word or two with Mrs Hallett. Then he'd go outside to see what the builders were doing. He often asked them questions about their work, but I'm not sure that their answers made him any the wiser.

We loved to stroll in the garden with Emily and Luther. Brian enjoyed looking at all the flowers and bushes, and he was particularly proud of his vegetable patch. He used to visit it a couple of times a day to talk to Mick or just to see by how much the vegetables had grown.

He often came running over to me with a carrot or some other similarly inspiring object in his hand.

'Anna, look! It's grown at least an inch!' he'd gush.

All this was new to him. He was exploring the world like a child. This was his first summer at Cotchford Farm and he enjoyed every minute.

Brian loved his new home, his house and his garden. There was only one thing that worried him — the stream. He often pointed out that we'd have to put up a fence so we needn't worry about our children falling in.

*   *   *

I was introduced to Frank Thorogood on my first Monday at the farm. My immediate impression of the builder was that he was a hard man, but he had a gentle face. He was in his mid-40s, tall and muscular with reddish-brown hair and a moustache. Brian had told me that Frank was married, but that he lived in the apartment above Brian's garage on weekdays.

I wasn't sure about Frank's position in the house when I first moved to Cotchford Farm. He behaved as if he owned the place, and I got the impression that Brian and Frank were old friends. After a couple of days, I asked Brian about Frank and he explained that Frank had been commissioned by Rolling Stones Incorporated to restore the farmhouse. Frank had been recommended by Tom Keylock, who was Frank's best friend, and before he arrived at the farm he'd done some work on Keith Richard's house, Redlands.

Keith never liked Frank and refused to let him into the house. Brian made the excuse that he needed male company and that's why he used to invite Frank in to have coffee, drinks and dinners.

'I know he's using me, but it's my own fault,' Brian said. 'I like having someone to chat to and Frank is better than no one.'

Occasionally I would be sunbathing while Brian and Frank were in the house, and I would often hear Brian roar with laughter. Eventually, curiosity made me venture into the dining room, where they usually sat drinking, to find out why. Generally, Brian would be in one of his boisterous moods, trying his best to make Frank loosen up. To my knowledge, he always failed.

'I wish I knew how to make Frank unwind,' Brian would say. 'I'd really enjoy making him lose his self-control — at least for once.'

'He's probably scared of making a fool of himself,' I said. 'Certain people need to be in control all the time.'

Brian didn't give up though. His wonderful, sunny smile made him look like an angel, but he was quite a mickey-taker and I soon realised that one of his favourite occupations was to tease Frank.

Frank took it personally. He couldn't see the funny side and he often sulked instead of shrugging his shoulders and letting it wash over him. I suspect he felt insulted and sometimes I thought that Brian went too far, especially when he pointed out to Frank that *he* was the boss, not Frank.

'If it weren't for me, you wouldn't have a job,' Brian might say. 'You should be grateful that I put food on your table.'

I should mention, however, that Frank never resisted paying Brian back. Sometimes I thought he went a bit too far when he attacked Brian and insulted him, such as the occasion when he said Brian was 'a spoilt, no-good rock star'.

'How in the world can you allow Frank to belittle you like that?' I asked Brian.

'It doesn't matter,' Brian said and shrugged. 'He knows I'm the master of the house and that he's dependent on me.'

In a battle of wits, Brian was superior. He was intelligent and well-read and Frank didn't stand a chance when Brian chose to dismiss him verbally. Frank knew this and he often came off the worst in their conversations.

When I was around, Brian and Frank showed off. They would sometimes have a go at Indian wrestling to prove their physical strength and they were cocky towards each other and me.

Compared to Brian, Frank was strong, but Brian offered stubborn resistance and sometimes he even won, much to Frank's displeasure.

*   *   *

It was only during my first week at Cotchford Farm that Frank tried to seduce me behind Brian's back. He put his arm around me and whispered that I ought to come to London with him. He always tried to hug and touch me when Brian wasn't around and he frequently tried to persuade me that he was the man I needed and that he could give me a far better life than Brian.

I didn't have the slightest interest in Frank. I found his advances unpleasant and embarrassing, due mostly to the fact that he, in my opinion, was an old duffer. He was twice my age, old enough to be my father.

To protect Brian, I didn't tell him what had been going on. I knew how sensitive and vulnerable he was and instead I chose to take Frank's hints as bad jokes.

But Frank enjoyed being mean to Brian and he knew all about his sore points, often using me to get at Brian.

'I'm thinking about bringing Anna back to London,' he would sometimes declare after enjoying a good meal at our expense.

'She's too young to be stuck down here in the middle of nowhere, right, Anna?'

I dismissed Frank's remarks but I could tell that Brian felt jealous and uneasy. It took him a while to pull himself together.

'You don't stand a chance,' he said to Frank eventually. 'You're an old man, your life is behind you. Anna's too young,' he continued with a wink, 'you don't have the strength to give her what she wants!'

Frank began to sulk and Brian laughed and called him a bad loser.

Even though Brian spent a lot of time with Frank, he also became quite angry with him occasionally.

'I'm quite sure that Frank is deliberately going slow with the work on the house. I mean, he's been here for eight months and the work's still not done. I don't know what the workmen are doing. Frank always comes up with some sort of explanation when I challenge him, but I don't know anything about restoring old houses so I can't contradict him. But I know he's cheating me. I bet ten to one that he's laughing behind my back.'

I agreed. Something didn't add up.

Brian said that Frank took advantage of him and, among other things, entertained his mistress on his property without his consent.

From time to time a woman by the name of Joan visited the house and chatted with Brian and Frank. I was naïve and thought that Joan was a friend of theirs, but one day when Brian had had enough of Frank, he told me that Joan was Frank's mistress and that Joan visited the apartment above the garage.

Brian became excited and his eyes flashed. I understood him. I didn't like the way Frank tried to get to Brian through me and when I got to know him better, I knew he was no friend of Brian's.

'You're just sitting around doing nothing!' Brian would shout at Frank. 'How much longer are you and your workmen going to be here? You're spending my money like water. I am sick of having you around all the time!'

When Brian let it all pour out I couldn't blame him. But Brian's anger soon disappeared and was replaced with pangs of conscience. He didn't like to fall out with anybody and whenever he'd shouted at Frank he always tried to smooth it over by inviting him in for a drink or dinner.

Frank could drink a considerable amount of alcohol. Most of the time he drank vodka, while Brian drank wine — or milk! And I didn't like the way Frank always tried to get Brian drunk. I still don't know why he'd do that.

I was also irritated by Frank's behaviour. He took it for granted that Brian would offer him dinner and drinks almost every day. I felt he should cook his own dinner. During the first weeks I was there, I didn't object, but when I began to find my feet I couldn't keep all my feelings to myself.

When I moved into Cotchford Farm everything was set up for a comfortable life. Every day one of the workmen went down to the grocery store in the village and shopped. But after a couple of weeks, I became suspicious when I heard Brian talking to the man who was going shopping. After a quick mental calculation it was obvious that the amount of food Brian was ordering would be enough for at least six people! I couldn't keep quiet.

'Are we having guests for dinner?' I asked when the workman had left the kitchen.

Brian looked perplexed and said that it was no more than usual.

'There are just the two of us,' I said. 'What happens to the rest of the food?'

I sat down at the kitchen table and told Brian that something suspicious was going on. Brian had never bothered to find out how much food was needed in a household and he'd never thought about the amount of groceries he ordered every day. The invoices were sent straight to Fred, the accountant at the Stones' office, so Brian never saw a bill. He hadn't even gone to the trouble of finding out how much housekeeping money he spent each month.

Together, we went through the fridges, freezers and larder. We cleaned out three or four mouldy cheeses, rancid butter, decomposed bacon and ham, a selection of ancient cooked meats and dozens of old eggs. We found at least 20 different marmalades and I felt that the time had come for me to speak my mind. At the same time, I took the opportunity to point out that it wasn't necessary to invite Frank to dinner every evening.

'I know,' Brian said. 'But I've treated him to dinner ever since he came to work here. I can't ask him to cook his own dinner now.'

Brian was generous and kind, sometimes to unreasonable extremes. On top of that, he was a bit of a coward and didn't dare tell Frank that he was no longer welcome for dinner. He was afraid that Frank would get upset with him.

Our stocktake prompted me to compose a new shopping list and I went down to the grocery store with the workman to see what it had to offer.

I wasn't the most popular woman in the area that day — and it got worse.

When I returned, I told Brian that I thought he was extravagant and irresponsible with money. He just smiled and was pleased that I wanted to take on the responsibility of the shopping.

I don't know if Frank used Brian's account for his own personal use, but I became suspicious one Friday evening when Brian and I were having dinner in the dining room, and we suddenly heard noises from outside the house.

I went to the front door and saw the workmen throwing armfuls of fresh vegetables into their cars. One of them saw me and put a finger to his lips. I immediately closed the door and went back to the dining room.

'What was all that about?' Brian asked.

'Some of the workmen are filling their cars with our vegetables,' I said.

Brian exploded in anger and rushed to the front door, opened it and stepped out onto the driveway.

'Who the hell told you you can take my vegetables?' he shouted.

One of the workmen turned to him. 'Frank told us to pick what we needed,' he said.

I thought Brian was going to burst a blood vessel; I'd never seen him so upset.

He shouted to the workmen to unload their cars and bring the vegetables to the kitchen door. They reluctantly obeyed him.

'If only they'd asked me, I would have given them as many vegetables as they wanted,' Brian said later. He felt annoyed and slighted by Frank.

'We have more than we need,' he went on. 'But the mere thought of people stealing vegetables ... how can anyone be so damn rude? And what the hell is wrong with Frank? He doesn't own the vegetables!'

I'm not sure whether Frank had really told the workmen to help themselves or if they'd just taken them given the opportunity. And I'm not sure if it was an isolated case or if it had been going on for some time.

But the memory of the incident aroused my suspicions about the groceries as well. From that day on, I handled the shopping myself and now and then I took Brian with me to help him understand how much we needed and how much we paid for it.

In a few weeks, I managed to halve the housekeeping costs, and Brian was very proud and pleased with me when Fred told him so.

But I don't think anyone else was.

*　　　*　　　*

I'd lived with Brian for about three weeks when I decided to return to London to pick up the rest of my belongings. I think I travelled back to London the same weekend Brian's parents came down to visit him, but I'm not sure.

It definitely coincided with Suki's mother coming down to fetch Matilda. Brian told me that Suki had gone to Morocco and that her mother had promised to take care of Matilda for her.

I will never forget the Thursday morning when I was leaving. Brian was worried and insisted that I take Emily with me to be quite sure that I'd come back.

He accompanied me to the taxi, hugged and kissed me and whispered, 'Please, hurry back. I miss you already.'

When I left, he sat on a rock in front of the house with Luther at his feet. He waved at me and I thought that he looked a bit lost. I almost told the driver to stop the taxi, but I resisted the urge.

I rang him four or five times during my stay in London and when I returned on the Sunday afternoon I saw Brian in the distance as we approached the house. He was sitting on the same rock as he had been when I left and Luther was lying at his feet. I was touched and my heart skipped — I found it both romantic and sweet.

Brian got up when he saw the taxi and greeted me with open arms and a big, welcoming smile. He helped me with my bags and boxes and told me he had a surprise waiting and quickly dragged me into the house.

The surprise was that he had prepared dinner — sausages and beans. He looked at me, proud and happy, and although I like neither sausages nor beans I tried to eat a little something to please him. He ate with a hearty appetite and beamed with contentment.

I think it was the first time he'd cooked anything which you could call a meal.

During my months at Cotchford Farm, I returned to London a couple of times to see my friends or just go shopping. Brian always sat on his favourite rock and waved farewell and he was overjoyed when I returned. I think that was the best part of my London visits — coming home to my beloved Brian.

*   *   *

In the mornings when Frank came into the kitchen to have a cup of coffee or tea, Brian would sometimes pick a quarrel with him just because he felt a bit out of sorts. He'd say something to Frank along the lines that his boys were working harder on the exterior of the house than they had done on the interior.

'And there's still nothing happening?' he'd shout. 'And you're just sitting here playing the gentleman. They must hate having you as a boss. See to it that they do a good job today — and you might be treated to a nice dinner tonight!'

Brian could tease people mercilessly and he enjoyed it when they were stung into submission. But he'd soon feel guilty and it wasn't long before he'd tell Frank that he didn't mean to upset him.

But I remember one particular day when nothing was going Brian's way. Frank was the one who had to put up with Brian's barracking.

'Tell me that you love me as a friend,' Brian began.

'I love you as a friend,' Frank said obediently.

'Tell me you will do anything I want,' Brian continued.

'You know I will do my best for you, Brian.'

'Tell me you have been negligent in the work you have done on the house.'

'I have been negligent,' Frank repeated, parrot-like.

'Tell me that everything is a complete shambles in the house.'

'Everything is a complete shambles in the house.'

'Tell me you want Anna,' Brian said.

'I want Anna,' Frank repeated.

'You can't have her,' Brian said flatly.

'Tell me that you're doing decent work for me.'

'I want Anna and I am doing my best for you,' Frank said.

Brian roared with laughter.

At times I found it hard to understand the fun in such games. Brian's humour was a bit odd. I asked him why he thought it was fun to make Frank embarrassed. Brian answered casually that he just wanted Frank to know his proper place.

Frank didn't understand music and was a little unworldly, or maybe he was just disinterested in things, something which Brian noticed particularly. Brian had travelled around the world and he'd had an eventful life. He was also curious and eager to learn. If he ran across something he wasn't familiar with, he always took his time to find out more about the subject. He was always keen to gain more knowledge and develop his skills.

It was beyond me why Brian persisted in his strained relations with Frank. The two of them had nothing in common and, anyway, Brian was unhappy with Frank's work. When I moved in there were at least two or three builders working on the exterior of the house. Frank never joined them. His contribution was merely to inspect their work now and then.

Brian continued to complain about the workmen and insisted that they just pretended to work and, of course, he blamed Frank. But Frank had dozens of excuses every time Brian questioned him and his workmen, and he was always ready to point out that Brian didn't know a damn thing about building or renovation. Brian listened to Frank and couldn't contradict him, but he was frustrated and said that he wished someone could prove that Frank wasn't doing his work properly.

In the last few weeks of his life, Brian contacted different builders and pretended he was the new owner of a house and asked them to come round and give him an estimate. I think one or two came to the house when Frank wasn't around, but Brian never received any estimates from them. At least, not while he was still alive.

*   *   *

After living at Cotchford Farm for about a month, I started to talk to Brian about the interior décor. If I was going to live there I felt that I needed the house to be warm and comfortable. I really wanted it to feel like a home.

I said to Brian that I thought the house was impersonal and that I wanted to redecorate it.

Brian was silent for a while then he asked me what I had in mind.

'I'd like to decorate one room at the time,' I said.

'I've already spent a fortune on the house,' he said slowly.

'Good taste doesn't have to be expensive,' I pointed out.

'OK,' he said at long last. 'We'll start going through the rooms one by one and you tell me what you want to change. But there's one room I want to decorate myself — our nursery!'

I agreed and thought he was sweet. I didn't mind about the nursery. We weren't going to have children for some time anyway. At least, that was what I thought.

Brian didn't agree with me on that subject. He was five years my senior, and he was more mature than me in many ways. He was ready to start a family with me and longed to be a father again. I, on the other hand, thought he rushed things.

But he made me change my mind.

CHAPTER SEVEN

BRIAN

Soon after moving in with Brian, I became aware of Brian's caution in and around water. I would lie by the swimming pool and sunbathe, and saw just how much Brian loved his pool and swimming in it. But he was very wary of the dangers around water and warned me never to jump into the pool if I was alone. If I felt like swimming, he wanted me to tell him in advance.

At first, I thought he was over-protective, a real mother hen, but as time passed it became quite normal for me to tell him. And Brian practices what he preached. He never swam alone and if we had guests at the house we always saw to it that one of us kept an eye on them if they were swimming.

After Brian's death I heard a rumour, which was said to have originated from Suki. Apparently, while he and Suki were spending the Christmas of 1968 in Ceylon, they went to a fortune-teller. Suki said that Brian had received a bizarre warning from the woman: 'Be careful swimming in the coming year. Don't go into the water without a friend.'

If it is true, it could explain Brian's concern. He never told me anything about his Christmas in Ceylon. The only thing I know is that Brian made sure that no one swam in the pool without supervision.

*   *   *

The summer of 1969 was the hottest I can remember in all my years in England and I spent most of my time in the garden while Brian was in the house chatting to Frank or playing in the music room. But he never left me on my own for long. At least every ten minutes he, Luther and sometimes Emily would come into the garden to make sure everything was all right.

Now and then I fancied strolling around the garden and Brian threw a fit if he couldn't see me. He always worried about me and he begged me to tell him if I wanted to go for a walk. He also wanted to know for how long I thought I would be away.

'If I finish my recording earlier than I thought it's nice to know where you are so I can catch up with you,' he said.

Sometimes, I found it a bit of a pain.

Like most people, I need to have a bit of space from time to time; to ponder, daydream, or just be alone. Brian was my absolute opposite. He always wanted to be close. I couldn't even go to the toilet alone. Brian would follow me into the bathroom and sit down by the toilet while I did what I had to do. Sometimes, I had to insist that I had a moment to myself.

The garden was my favourite place. It was beautiful and peaceful and I particularly loved to wander about in the rose garden and enjoy the beautiful blooms.

The garden, with its arbour and terraces, was special and Brian told me about a young woman who had once worked as a maid in the house and who had been buried in the garden. He didn't know where, but he was convinced that it was true. He said that he'd seen and heard her. I think her Christian name was Mary, just like Mrs Hallett's.

Brian said that Mary had been a restless soul and that he had tried to help her find peace. He had invited a few guests to Cotchford Farm, among them Marianne Faithful and John Lennon. The hashish billowed like a mist in the house as they played the music from Jajouka and said prayers for her. The party had been going on for several days and Brian said that he'd neither seen her nor heard her since then.

Maybe she'd got tried of listening to the music and the prayers and moved out!

I couldn't blame the hashish for making Brian believe that Mary had gone. Brian didn't smoke when I met him, not even ordinary cigarettes. He didn't like it that I was a smoker and often lectured me about the effect on my health. I tried to ignore him.

Brian enjoyed the garden as much as me, but he was too restless to enjoy the sun. When he was in the garden, we usually wandered about or swam in the pool. During the weekends, when we were not disturbed by Frank or the workmen, we often skinny-dipped and enjoyed being alone. Sometimes, we swam in the evenings when darkness had fallen.

The garden was beautiful at night. The pool was lit by floodlights and shimmered invitingly. It was almost like living in fairyland and I wouldn't have been surprised if I'd seen a fairy dance on the terraces, or a gnome strolling about in the garden.

Brian often said that the garden looked like an advertising poster for Hollywood.

'But it's much more beautiful here,' he said, 'much more beautiful.'

We swam and played in the turquoise water. Brian loved to show off. He swam like a fish and tried to teach me different styles, like the butterfly stroke for instance, but I couldn't get the hang of it. Brian told me that he'd entered competitions when he was younger and I believed him. I loved to watch him dive from the springboard, revelling in his ability in the water. It seemed to me that water was his natural element. He was at one with it.

I miss our evenings in the pool. We had some wonderful times there. Just the two of us — and the dogs.

*   *   *

In my eyes, Brian was a mature man. He had accomplished his dreams in his own way. He had bought his dream house with its beautiful garden, swimming pool and vegetable patch. He had two dogs and a cat, who appeared in the kitchen from time to time when it was hungry, and now he longed to start a family and become a father again.

Brian often told me that he wished I was older. He was five years older than me, but sometimes the difference in age seemed to be greater. Brian had had an eventful life, whereas I was both inexperienced and naïve.

I'd never witnessed the demons that supposedly haunted Brian, as some people said. They'd probably disappeared when he gave up drugs, and I never had a lecture about Satan, which, according to his friends, was a favourite topic earlier on. On the contrary, he loved to tell stories about good-natured ghosts who walked the earth after their death. Brian believed in an after-life and sometimes I wonder if it is Brian who scratches my back and leads me into the dream world. Who knows? He was a firm believer.

One of his most characteristic features was his impulsiveness.

One day, without any reason, he came running towards me and swept me up into his arms.

'I want us to buy a car,' he said. 'What do you want?'

At first I thought he meant a car with a chauffeur and I said that it wasn't necessary.

'We don't need a car,' I said. 'And it'll be expensive paying for a chauffeur.'

'We *definitely* need a car,' Brian said, 'But we don't need a chauffeur. I'd like a Mercedes, like Mick's. A white Mercedes.'

'Let's think about it for a while,' I said. 'We're in no hurry, are we?' Brian was impressed by Mick Jagger's white Mercedes and thought it was one of the nicest cars around.

I didn't seem able to convince Brian that we didn't need a car, as he'd set off to ring Fred at the Stones' office to order one.

'Tell me what kind of car you want!' he shouted over his shoulder.

'I don't want a car,' I said. 'I want a bicycle!'

The next morning, a new bicycle was propped up outside the front door.

I learned to live with Brian's impulsiveness and I often teased him about it. I remember some evenings when he would recount his adventures in Morocco, and he'd get so carried away he'd ring his friend Brion Gysin. They'd talk for a while and then Brian would say he wanted to visit him. When he'd eventually hung up, he'd turn to me.

'I'll order the plane tickets,' he'd say excitedly. 'Why don't you pack a suitcase in the meantime?'

He always told me to pack white clothes. All other colours were forbidden. The only non-white item he accepted was my black bikini.

When I'd finished packing, I'd go down to Brian — who would probably have already changed his mind. I don't know how many times I had to cancel air tickets and unpack clothes.

The morning after every 'journey', I used to give him a kiss when we woke up and whisper teasingly, 'Where have we been? Was it Morocco? Or maybe Portugal?'

Sometimes when I think about Brian it gives me a deep pain. I miss his closeness, his warmth. I miss our nights together.

Brian would often wake up in the middle of the night and hug me until I woke up.

'I'm so happy I met you,' he'd whisper. 'I just wanted to make sure you're still here.'

I loved sleeping next to Brian. He made me feel safe and often, when he thought I was asleep, he'd search for my hand and bring it to his lips and kiss it. Our lovemaking was tender and frequent. We could doze and still make love. It was like being in a dreamland.

Brian was easy to get along with and he made me laugh. Sometimes he could lift me up in the air and whirl me around until my head would spin and then we'd fall into each other's arms and laugh with joy. But, of course, we also had our fair share of mundane, day-to-day living.

It was not long before we eased into our daily routines. Breakfast in the morning, afternoon tea and dinner in the evening. A stroll in the garden, a trip in the car Brian had bought for Mick Martin, an hour or two in the music room, sunbathing by the pool and TV at night. We lived a quiet and relaxing life and I couldn't have been happier.

We spent hours in the music room. Brian knew someone in London who'd send him all the new singles and albums. He always played them and listened attentively to see if the artist appealed to him. If it didn't catch his interest he never played it again. It would be sorted away into the collection.

Bob Dylan, Richie Havens and Credence Clearwater Revival were Brian's absolute favourites that summer of 1969. He played their records over and over again, concentrating on how the instruments were played and listening to the lyrics.

'Credence Clearwater Revival is the best thing to have hit the music industry for a long time,' Brian said. 'They play the kind of music I want to play and they remind me of the music we played in the Stones when we first started out.'

Brian and I both loved music and we played together now and then. I'd learned to play the piano at an early age and I also play flute, trumpet, cornet and balalaika. When I told Brian I could play the balalaika he was thrilled and wanted me to teach him. He'd never played the balalaika himself and he was curious. I also got him interested in the accordion and we decided to buy one as soon as possible.

I'd always dreamed about playing the saxophone — Brian started out as a saxophonist — and sometimes I'd sneak down into the music room when Brian was asleep to try to learn how to play it. There's something profoundly raw about it, and it's just about the sexiest instrument ever made. At least, that's what I think.

Brian was always searching for new sounds and he would continue looking until he found the particular sound he wanted. Sometimes he found it immediately, and sometimes it took ages. Usually he knew what it should sound like, but he didn't know which instrument to use.

Brian was a perfectionist. He was never satisfied until he'd discovered the perfect sound. And when he found it, he was as happy as could be and rang his friends to share his success.

Every now and then, he came running out into the garden.

'I want you to listen to something and tell me what you think,' he'd garble.

I'd follow him to the music room and he'd play a new tune or a recording.

'What do you think?' he'd usually ask. 'Do you like it?'

I was honest, most of the time, but Brian was sensitive and

when he was in a particular mood I'd have to think carefully before speaking, especially if I wasn't immediately won over by it.

Sometimes, Brian would wake me up in the middle of the night when he thought he'd found a way to get a sound he wanted.

'Anna, Anna! I've just worked out how to play it. Come on ... I want you to hear it!'

I'd be half asleep when he'd take my hand and lead me down the stairs to the music room, but his joy and enthusiasm were catching.

Brian's inspiration flowed unstemmed during the months I lived with him and he taped many new compositions and sounds. But he didn't record a single, which he was said to have done before he died. Brian would probably have recorded his compositions some time or other. But none of the compositions were finished and he hadn't written any lyrics.

*   *   *

Brian and I could often spend days in the music room and in the tape room listening to and sorting out his recordings. We used to sit on the floor and Brian would tell me who he was playing with and when he'd taped the session and how much fun they'd had doing it.

In the bedroom, we always listened to Brian's favourite albums, which he'd bring with him when we were going to bed. He always wanted to listen to music when he was about to fall asleep. If the record finished before he'd nodded off, he used to crawl over me and play it again from the beginning.

For quite a long period, we fell asleep to Bob Dylan's *Nashville Skyline* and Brian used to sing the song 'To Be Alone with You' softly in my ear and hold me tight.

THE POOL

To be alone with you
Just you and me
Now won't you tell me true
Ain't that the way it oughta be?
To hold each other tight
The whole night through
Ev'rything is always right
When I'm alone with you

To be alone with you
At the close of the day
With only you in view
While evening slips away
It only goes to show
That while life's pleasures be few
The only one I know
is when I'm alone with you.

They say that night-time is the right time
To be with the one you love
Too many thoughts get in the way in the day
But you're always what I'm thinkin' of
I wish the night were here
Bringin' me all of your charms
When only you are near
To hold me in your arms

I'll always thank the Lord
When my working day's through
I get my sweet reward
To be alone with you.

We both loved this particular Dylan album. Its happy feel was infectious. My favourite track was 'Lay, Lady, Lay' and of course 'To Be Alone With You'.

We fell asleep to music and awoke to music. The first thing Brian did on waking was to play a record; music was ever-present.

Sometimes I forgot about the albums which lay scattered by my side of the bed and I often came close to stepping on them, but apart from the records Brian was generally quite tidy. It is true that when he undressed he made a pile of clothes on the floor, but it was just one pile. He never spread his clothes or anything else around the room.

Even though music was a significant part of our lives, we hardly ever talked about Brian's work with the Stones. Our discussions were usually about what we thought of life in general. We often discussed politics and when I had an outburst he always smiled.

'Do you know how cute you are when you're upset about all the injustice in the world?' he used to say.

When he smiled I soon calmed down and I couldn't stop myself from laughing.

Brian always let me know that he loved me. He never hesitated to show his affection. When I look back, I wish I had made him understand how much he meant to me, how much I loved him, that he was the man in my life. He gave me so much, much more than I gave him in return.

But even if I didn't tell Brian I loved him as often as I wish I'd done, I knew that we belonged together. He was my man, and I was his woman, those feelings being just as strong as when I first laid eyes on him.

During the five years that passed since our first meeting, Brian had become tired of the rock 'n' roll lifestyle and I'd had my chance to mature. That treadmill of visiting the clubs, meeting people from all walks of life, having several boyfriends and leading a fairly hedonistic existence was well and truly behind me.

Now we were both ready to commit ourselves to our love.

CHAPTER EIGHT

THE CLOTHES

BRIAN

When people talk about Brian they often mention his clothes. Brian had an acute dress sense and was aware of how people would look at him. As I mentioned earlier, the dominant pieces of furniture in his bedroom and bathroom were his wardrobes. I don't remember how many he had, but it must have been at least ten, and they were all filled with clothes, hats and shoes.

Brian loved white suits and several of the wardrobes contained suits of different styles and makers. When we started going out together, he was always smartly dressed. He preferred jackets or suits and he always wore multicoloured scarves, one around his hat and one around his neck. He had hundreds of them in different colours and patterns.

Brian also loved his hats and had a huge selection of various styles and colours. And then there were his shoes. I don't think I've ever seen so many shoes before or since, except in shoe shops.

But the coolly dressed Brian, whom I'd got to know in London, disappeared at Cotchford Farm. When I moved in with him, I tended to regard him as scruffy and completely disinterested in looking smart.

'What d'you think I should wear today?' he asked me every morning. Why, I still don't understand.

At first, I thought he wanted me to help him choose from his crammed wardrobes and I used to pick out trousers and smart tops or shirts, but it always ended with him putting on a multicoloured shirt or a T-shirt, his shabby beige trousers or shorts and a pair of worn-out shoes.

Occasionally, I forced him to put on something else, but he loved strolling around in his favourite clothes, relaxing and forgetting that he was a rock star. It didn't matter — he was handsome to look at whatever he wore.

When Brian and I began dating I'd had my long, dark hair cut and bleached. I liked it and so did Brian, although he preferred long hair. He often laughed and said that it was easy to mistake me for him when I was swimming in the pool. Brian was not particularly tall either. He was about 175 centimetres (5ft 9in), ten centimetres taller than me.

One evening, Brian took my hand and we went up to the bedroom where he opened his wardrobes and started rooting among the clothes. Then he gave me a couple of white suits.

'Try them on!' he said.

He lay down on the bed and watched me modelling the suits. Several of them fitted me and I finally found one that was perfect. Brian laughed and said that I looked exactly like him.

'The suits seem to be made for you,' he said. 'You look like a genuine tomboy!'

After that first night, we often dressed up. I'd put on one of Brian's suits and play the man, and Brian would dress as a woman. I'd back-comb his hair and put it up or tie it in a ponytail with a big ribbon. But he preferred doing his make-up himself and, to tease me, he always stood in front of the wardrobe doors when he painted his eyelashes. The mascara spattered the mirror, just as it did when I painted my eyelashes!

Brian enjoyed seeing me in his clothes. He loved lying on the bed with Emily at his side while I paraded in front of him.

'You look just like me,' he said contentedly. 'The suits look good on you. You're gorgeous!'

Some evenings we would go through all the wardrobes and Brian would want me to try on one outfit after another. I think I turned him on when I wore his clothes and I know he loved to seduce me and undress me until I was standing in front of him wearing nothing but my lace underwear.

He often said that he'd never met a girl with such beautiful underwear and every now and then I'd see him walking by the clothesline casually brushing against my silk underwear.

Although Brian loved to see me modelling his clothes, he was reluctant to dress up himself. If I hadn't forced him, he would gladly have skipped the shower as well.

Now I understand that it was freeing for him not to have to think about his appearance all the time. At the farm, he could be himself and put the fashion-conscious rock star image behind him. And if that meant wearing comfortable, scruffy clothes, then so be it.

*   *   *

I believe the time Brian and I spent together was one of the best periods of his life. He had said goodbye to the trappings of rock stardom and he was looking forward to his new drug-free life.

He told me once that his dream had been to play in the greatest rock 'n' roll band in the world and that he hadn't thought about what the consequences of this dream would be.

Success made him both jealous and envious, he'd said. He'd lost himself in the fame and after a while he started to believe in the image of himself. He thought he was Superman. Everything he did was intensified and he gave the press exactly what they wanted — he practically wrote the headlines himself.

But by the time we'd hooked up together, he'd turned his back on his old habits and had his future ahead of him. He'd started his new life and I was a part of it.

We were happy at Cotchford Farm and we had no need for company in the first month or so. We were enjoying the everyday routine and we went off on short trips in the beautiful countryside surrounding the farm. We went down to the pub in the local village or visited others nearby.

Brian drove the car, but he wasn't a terribly good driver since he had trouble concentrating. Instead, he'd enjoy the lush, green landscape or talk to me in the passenger seat. One day, he didn't notice another car suddenly appear from the left and which had right of way. Brian had to slam on the brakes and we narrowly escaped a horrific collision.

It shocked both of us and Brian couldn't stop talking about it. He said that he was a worthless driver and that he shouldn't be allowed to drive. He continued on that theme all the way home. And later that night, he found he couldn't sleep for fear of what might have happened.

'What if something had happened to you?' he said. 'What if you'd been badly wounded or even died? I wouldn't have had anything left to live for, would I?'

If I remember correctly, it was only the next day when we learned that Anita and Keith had crashed their car at about the same time as we'd had our narrow escape. We'd also learned that Anita was pregnant. Brian's reaction to the news was spiteful, to say the least.

His conscience got the better of him an hour or so later,

though, and he asked me to write a card to Anita and wish her well with her baby. He didn't mention Keith.

Children and animals were very close to Brian's heart. He never missed an opportunity to talk proudly about his sons, and Luther and Emily were always at his side. Brian loved all animals and it wasn't just idle talk. He proved it to me one day when we were driving around. Suddenly we saw a black cat laying motionless in the middle of the road. Brian hit the brakes and jumped out, and I followed him. It turned out that the cat was still alive.

'How can anyone run over a cat and leave it?' Brian said, horrified. 'Some people don't have any feelings at all!'

Brian gently lifted the cat up and carried it to the car where he carefully placed it on the back seat. Then he drove to the nearest vet. Having explained what had happened, he offered to pay for the treatment.

Over the following few days, Brian called the surgery several times to ask after the cat. It slowly came round and the vet was convinced it would be all right. He also promised to see to it that the cat went to a good home, if they didn't succeed in their search for the owner.

It wasn't until the vet had made that promise that Brian could relax and stop worrying about the cat.

*   *   *

Brian and I were deeply in love and at first there was no room for anyone else in our lives. We just enjoyed the simplicity of our new life together. Brian was romantic and attentive. He picked me a bouquet of roses from the rose garden or read me a romantic love poem.

Often, when we sneaked back to bed after lunch, Brian brought a collection of poems which he'd read aloud. At other times, he'd read something from *Winnie the Pooh* or the Bible. He knew the Old Testament well and loved reading it, and I enjoyed listening to him. Brian had an ability to bring the books he read alive even if I didn't understand every word.

Brian seemed so happy, busying himself with his music, his reading and his beloved garden.

I can still see him in my mind's eye, strolling around the garden, bending down now and then to pull up a weed or a leaf from the lawn. Sometimes he bore an uncanny resemblance to Christopher Robin in his shorts and hat, and their hairstyles were almost identical.

I was also charmed by the house and the beautiful garden. It really was a bewitching fairyland.

When I sat outside in the summer nights, I wouldn't have been the least surprised if I'd seen Winnie the Pooh or Christopher Robin mooching about in the shadows.

Brian often told me that he was going to live at Cotchford Farm for ever. He said it was his first true home since he'd moved away from his parents. He didn't count the apartments he'd lived in, saying that they never felt like home.

*   *   *

I knew that Brian's friends were curious about me. It was clear from several telephone conversations Brian had had that he didn't mind telling them about me. He wanted everyone to know I was his girlfriend and that we lived together, but at the same time he didn't want to tell anyone too much about me. He wasn't that kind of a person; he wanted to keep his private life private.

One of the first to learn that Brian and I were living together was Bill Wyman, whose girlfriend, Astrid, was also Swedish. Brian rang him one day and proudly announced that he, too, had a girlfriend from Sweden. And I guess Bill told the other

Me in 1967 on tour with the Swedish dance group The Ravens.

The girl who tried to save Brian Jones

Top: This portrait was taken shortly after Brian's death.

Bottom left: Me with Frank Thorogood. I found consolation wearing Brian's hat, and Frank lent me a coat to protect me from the crowd who disliked my dress.

Bottom right: Leaving the Londonderry Hotel for the inquest with publicist David Sandison. This is the dress that was too much for the British press – they jeered and taunted me.

Ravenswood
335 Hatherley Road
Cheltenham
Glos
1.12.69

Dear Anna,

I was so pleased to hear from you after such a long time and I must apologise for being so long in replying.

It meant a great deal to me to understand that Brian was so happy during his last few weeks of his life.

There are many things I do not understand about the terrible night he died, and about the way he died.

But I shall always be grateful for what you tried to do. You failed to save his life, he had been in the water too long, but I believe you really did try. I have no idea how long he was done, but it must have been a long time, because he was such a good swimmer.

Of course you may go to his grave anytime you wish. You do not need my permission nor anyone else's. ~~Plea~~. People have been from all over the world.

I too was a little surprised you did not come to his funeral, but I just thought you wanted to go home after your ordeal.

Well, Good Bye for now Anna, thank you so much for writing.

Very sincerely
Lewis Jones

A kind letter from Brian's father, Lewis.

Posing as a 'Raven'. I also performed on TV shows as one of the troupe.

Top: The swimming pool at Cotchford Farm where Brian met his tragic end.

Bottom: Visiting Brian's grave – it is always an emotional moment.

Top: A happy reunion! Brian's housekeeper Mrs Hallet and I reminisce.

Bottom: A wave for the camera! Me aged two with my parents.

The statue of Christopher Robin had pride of place in the garden at Cotchford Farm.

A portrait of me taken in 1970. Although Brian and I shared wonderful times, the horror and trauma of what happened that night in 1969 will stay with me forever.

members of the Stones what the situation was.

We enjoyed the tranquility of our little idyll, but I knew that, sooner or later, it would be shattered — and it was — by Tom Keylock and his friends.

It all began one evening when Tom called from London to say that he was on his way down to Cotchford Farm with four mates. Brian was surprised and couldn't find a way of putting him off.

Tom reminded me of Frank, and I could see why the two of them were friends. They were the same kind of people. He sat down and poured wine into Brian's glass as soon as it was empty. Brian got very drunk.

He then turned his attention to me and asked me about my life with Brian.

'Why are you staying here?' he asked. 'Come with me to London. I'll see to it that you get work as a model. As a matter of fact we're planning a movie. Maybe you'd like to be one of the girls?'

I smiled and said that I wasn't interested. Today, I still don't understand why Frank and Tom kept asking that I should go back to London. They both knew that Brian was irritated by their suggestions and they were aware of his insecurity about my leaving him. They both probably just enjoyed teasing him.

I kept my cool and when Tom and the others had turned away, I poured the drinks out. I didn't like the atmosphere in the room. It made me feel uncomfortable.

Brian became more drunk by the minute and I felt it was time for Tom and his friends to move on, which I told them. They ignored me and when we'd had enough, Brian and I left them in the music room.

It was the first time I'd seen Brian helplessly drunk and I had to drag him upstairs to bed. I lay down beside him and tried to sleep. I'd dozed off when I suddenly heard someone open the bedroom door. I don't know who it was but the intruder tried to drag me back down to the music room. I hissed at him and he disappeared.

I suppose Tom and his friends had wanted to visit Brian and have a pleasant evening, and I guess that they, or at least Tom, were curious about me. They probably thought I was naïve and might be easily impressed by their talk about helping me get a job as a model. I didn't like any of them, especially Tom, who affected an unpleasant air of superiority.

I had a sleepless night. I dozed off now and then, but Brian's snoring soon woke me up. Finally, I'd had enough and with Emily at my heels, went into the guest room next to our bedroom to try to get some sleep. Remarkably, Brian woke up after a while and followed me. He woke me with caresses and kisses and begged me to come back to the bedroom.

'I can't sleep when you're not there,' he whispered. 'Please, come back to bed.'

I knew I'd give in if I turned over and saw his beautiful smile and imploring look, and sure enough, I couldn't resist him. I followed him back to the bedroom again — and Brian fell contentedly to sleep and began to snore ...

The following morning, we overslept. Tom and his friends were still around, and kept on about my going to London. It wasn't long before Brian fell out with Tom.

'I didn't invite you!' Brian yelled. 'This isn't a hotel where you and Frank can behave like idiots. Clear out! Now!'

Tom said nothing, but smiled at Brian. He didn't react immediately, it was as if he was weighing up all of Brian's weak points. Brian, on the other hand, looked as if he was about to explode. Then he turned and asked me to follow him out into the garden.

'If anyone is going to take your picture it's David Bailey,' he said.

David Bailey, the world-famous photographer, was a friend of

Brian's. I'd never met him, but Brian talked about him a lot and we were planning to go to Portugal with him and his girlfriend in August that year.

When Tom and his companions had departed at long last, Brian didn't budge from my side. He was terribly upset and worried himself sick imagining that I'd believed Tom and his talk about a career as a model.

'If you really want to give it a try and make some money, I'll help you,' he said. 'But, please, don't listen to Tom. He can't do anything for you, he's just trying to make an impression on you.'

I was neither interested in money nor a career and I tried to explain my feelings to Brian. I enjoyed my peaceful, happy life with him — until I saw a completely new and frightening side to the man I loved.

*   *   *

Brian was a complex personality. He was irresistibly charming, kind-hearted, cheerful, amusing, funny, curious, energetic and moral, but also cynical, wicked, annoying, lazy, weak, nervous, restless, aggressive and menacing. He was also a dreamer and a seeker.

I will always miss the closeness and the safety I felt in Brian's presence. He'd often sneak up behind me and put his arms around me before he whirled me around and kissed me, and I will always miss our nights when we slept together with our legs entwined, holding hands.

To my mind, Brian and I were soul-mates. We laughed, cried, joked and enjoyed the same things. We could talk about all or nothing for hours. We could sit quietly and just enjoy being together, or listen to music and play instruments together. Our life was a dream come true, except for one dark cloud in our sky — Brian's jealously.

I don't know why Brian was jealous. Maybe it was due to his insecurity. His jealousy was ever-present and showed itself in various ways. He also tried to make me jealous by using one of his female friends, Amanda Lear.

'Amanda wants to visit me,' he said once when he was talking on the phone. 'Do you mind?'

'No,' I said. 'Why should I?'

Brian looked surprised and later he asked me why I wasn't jealous. He couldn't understand it.

He tried the same thing several times. Now and then my lack of jealousy made him so upset that he couldn't sleep. He would wake me up in the middle of the night demanding an explanation as to why I wasn't jealous and I told him that there was nothing to discuss.

'I'm just trying to make you jealous,' he sulked.

'Sorry, wrong method,'

'You don't love me,' he'd say, and turn his back on me.

I explained that I didn't have the right to determine what he should or shouldn't do.

'If you want to invite your friends, it's up to you,' I said. 'I don't mind.'

But, to be honest, I did feel a twinge of jealousy.

After a while, he settled down and fell asleep next to me and when the morning came, he would have forgotten about the incident. Until the next time.

When the boot was on the other foot, though, Brian reacted quite differently.

One day, the telephone rang when I was in the garden. I went into the house with Brian close behind. The call was from Victor Lownes, the owner of Playboy Club, and one of my closest friends. He was also one of the few who knew I was living with Brian. He invited Brian and me to a party and we continued to gossip about what was going on in London.

Then without any warning, Brian exploded with rage. He ripped the telephone flex from the wall and pushed me forcibly up against the fridge. He was mad with jealousy and I was convinced that he would hit me. I started to quake with fear. I'd never seen Brian like this before and it scared me. I was completely unprepared. Victor had only been trying to be nice.

'What the hell do you think you're doing?' I shouted and managed to break free from his hold. The only thing I could think about was getting away from him, fast.

I ran upstairs and threw some clothes into a bag and rang for a taxi. Eventually, a sheepish and remorseful Brian came up to the bedroom. He begged my forgiveness and started to cry. He said he'd thought I was going to leave him and the mere suggestion had driven him to despair.

Brian had got it into his head that I didn't want him any more, and that I'd longed to go back to my friends in London. He fell on to his knees with tears streaming down his cheeks.

'Please, Anna! Don't go. Stay with me. I can't go on living without you. Anna, I love you. Please forgive me. Tell me you'll stay?'

I thought long and hard, unpacked my bag cancelled the taxi, but only once he'd sworn that he'd never lay a hand on me again ... ever.

In spite of his solemn promise, it wasn't long before he'd have another outburst — but looking back, I understand why it happened.

CHAPTER NINE

THE

DRUGS

Brian didn't use any drugs when I lived with him at Cotchford Farm. His doctor had prescribed Mandrax to help him sleep, and Valium, which he needed from time to time and, of course, he had his inhaler for his asthma.

However, I never saw him under the influence of any of these drugs. Brian was scared of drugs, preferring his white wine. Generally, he drank a bottle of Blue Nun, but I only saw him drunk on two occasions.

We often talked about Brian's earlier experiences with drugs. He was well aware that he had almost ruined his life because of drug abuse, and he wasn't the only one. In the Sixties, drugs were a part of our culture, our day-to-day existence. We lived on cannabis, uppers, downers and free love. Most of us didn't know how dangerous it was, or we were able to keep the drug-popping under control.

When I first met Brian he wanted to stay away from drugs. He was terrified that the police would bust him again at his home and because of that he only took his prescribed medication, and then only rarely.

'1967, when the police busted me, I woke up,' Brian said. 'They scared the shit out of me. It was horrible and I decided there and then never to touch drugs after that.'

Brian kept his promise, but a year later he was busted again. The police had apparently found some cannabis in a stocking in his apartment. Brian was very upset about this.

'I honestly don't know who put the hash in my flat,' he said. 'It didn't belong to me. Someone must have put it in the drawer and rung the police. Why else would they raid the flat when I hadn't been living there for ages?'

Brian often talked about the ordeal he went through when he was busted and how relieved he was when he was allowed to leave custody.

'When I was released I was taken to a hotel until the trial,' Brian said. 'It wasn't much better. I still felt like a prisoner.'

The only people he saw were the ones who were hired by the Rolling Stones.

'I'm sure they took advantage of me,' Brian said. 'I had to pay double the price for everything I ordered and I reckon I had to pay for their drinks, food and fags as well. It was one of the worst periods of my life and I swore that I'd never put myself through that again.'

His last confrontation with the police, a year later, made Brian decide to get away from London. He was convinced that the police would bust him continually if he stayed on in his flat.

He was probably right. Brian and other rock stars at that time were made examples of. Today, they probably wouldn't get busted at all for the small quantities of cannabis they often have. Looking back, I think that the whole thing was unnecessary. It wasn't as if Brian had used heroin or other hard drugs. He wasn't a junkie, as he often pointed out.

'I'd never give myself a shot,' he said. 'It's disgusting and I can't understand why people stick needles into themselves.'

Brian told me a few things about him and Anita and their life together. He said that the two of them had not really experienced a normal, everyday life, having frequently been under the influence of drugs. Brian and Anita were considered a 'trendy', hedonistic couple. Brian was convinced that the drugs enabled them to enjoy a fantasy lifestyle. While they took drugs everything was beautiful and they dressed in silk, velvet and other sumptuous fabrics.

'Some days we could stand in front of the mirror for hours admiring ourselves. We thought we were two of the most important people in the world and that we were the only ones that mattered.

'We were the king and the queen of the Sixties. We were rich and beautiful and we never considered the consequences of our actions.'

Brian never forgave himself for the picture which was taken of him dressed up in a Nazi uniform. He was under the influence of LSD at the time and hadn't thought about the repercussions until it was too late.

'That picture was for private use,' he said. 'It wasn't meant to be public. I was too stoned to realise that the photographer had other plans.

'I can only really blame myself and my stupidity at the time.'

The photographer knew there was money to be made and contacted the newspapers, and Brian was destroyed when the picture was published. He felt let down.

'I was an emotional mess when I lived with Anita,' Brian admitted, 'both as a musician and as a boyfriend. Everyone was spaced out and the drugs did nothing but cause trouble. Lots of the things we did under the influence of drugs were really bad.'

Brian said he'd learnt his lesson the hard way, and that he wouldn't dwell on the past. He looked to the future with confidence.

'When you're under the influence of drugs you never know who your true friends are,' Brian said. 'But you *believe* that everyone is your best friend. Until you wake up.'

I know Brian made great demands upon his true friends. Most of them were clever, witty and honest. There was no bullshit, as Brian put it. All the others were mere acquaintances, people who used him for their own ends.

*   *   *

When Brian talked about Anita he was often very negative and he claimed that their relationship was a disaster.

'Our life together was a constant see-saw between drugs and fights,' he said. 'We were always competing with each other for the most attention. It didn't matter whether we were hated or admired, just getting the attention was the main thing.'

It seems that Anita brought out the worst in Brian and I suspect that he in return tried his best to offend, hurt her and have the last word. Presumably, she felt she needed to defend herself. As I see it, it was a constant struggle between the two of them and they both tried to emerge victorious.

In spite of the drugs and the frequent fights, I'm convinced that Brian loved Anita. And I know he saw her in me. Maybe there was a sort of similarity between the two of us, but we were hardly twins.

I particularly remember one evening when we were having dinner with Frank, when Brian turned to him and started talking about Anita.

'Doesn't Anna remind you of Anita?' Brian asked. Frank, of course, agreed.

I didn't want to be compared with Anita, and Brian's question awakened my slumbering jealousy.

'Don't compare me with Anita,' I hissed. 'I am *me*, not Anita!'

'I know, Anna,' Brian said and smiled. 'That's why you live with me and she doesn't. My life is peaceful at last — and I owe it to you.'

I struggled to come to terms with his comments, but deep down, I was deeply hurt.

Brian later admitted that he had been completely controlled by Anita and although he realised that their relationship had been destructive and doomed to failure, he couldn't leave her.

'I've never met a woman who has exerted such influence over me,' Brian admitted. 'I can't explain why, but I wouldn't be surprised if she has some kind of magic powers.

'Perhaps she's a witch,' he added. 'A real witch.'

I laughed at him, and he sulked. I'm convinced, though, that they were both to blame for their confused relationship. The one thing I find difficult to understand is the way Anita broke up with Brian, leaving him in Morocco, while she, without much explanation, returned to England with Keith and Tom Keylock.

I tried to look at it from Brian's perspective and understand his anger and sense of loss, and I knew months went by before the pain had passed. But when we got together at long last he was a happy, vital young man. I only ever saw him depressed on one occasion — when he quit the Stones. To me, he was one, big, sunny smile.

*　　　　　*　　　　　*

Brian's asthma had been the cause of much speculation. I'm aware that he always made a point of having his inhaler handy and some days he used it, but he never had an attack of asthma in my presence and the illness didn't worry him that much. He was used to it and he knew how to handle it.

What worried him more was drugs. He was relieved not to have ended up addicted to heroin like Anita, Keith and Marianne Faithfull.

'I'm not sure, but I suspect I once had heroin,' Brian told me one night. 'I remember I was stoned out of my head and lying in my apartment when somebody gave me a shot. I thought it felt nice at the time, but I'd never give myself another shot.'

Brian dissociated himself from heroin, thinking the drug to be awful. On that subject, he told me about Marianne Faithfull, whom he had known before she met Mick Jagger.

'She was a nice, beautiful girl, but the heroin nearly destroyed her and I don't want to have anything to do with either her or Anita. I find it difficult to accept their drug abuse.

'I know it's hard to get off the drugs. I still have my ups and downs and I only used acid [LSD] and smoked a joint now and then. But I realise now that drugs are an escape and I don't want to run the risk of ending up like I was before, or like some of my former friends. That's why I try not to give in when I long for something.'

I never saw Brian take any drugs apart from Valium and Mandrax. I guess his earlier experiences had made him a bit restless and he took his Valium to help him relax, but not on a regular basis and never in combination with drinks or when he was swimming.

Brian was scared of the habit-forming medication and didn't want to be too dependent on them. But at the same time he was also aware of his looks and that he'd gained a couple of pounds, which worried him. That was the reason he contacted his doctor shortly before he died and asked for some slimming tablets. He gave him Durophet, also known as 'black bombers', and the prescription was for ten tablets.

At the time Brian made the call, I had about 100 Durophet,

which my doctor had prescribed for me, but I didn't dare tell him. I used Durophet and Mandrax secretively. I wasn't dependent, but I liked to have a trip occasionally, but to be on the safe side I never mixed drugs and drinks.

After Brian's death, someone said that when I moved in with him, Brian had opened my bags and made sure that I didn't bring any drugs into his house. That's not so. Brian never even asked me if I used drugs, but something must have made him suspicious.

One morning, when I overslept, I was roughly awakened by Brian, who had grabbed my hair and was dragging me into the bathroom. Still drowsy, I saw him empty all my pills on to the bathroom floor. When he'd finished, he hit and hugged me indiscriminately while he was yelling at me. I'd never seen him so furious. Finally, he pushed me down onto the floor and his eyes spat fire.

'What the hell do you think you're doing? Are you out of your mind? Don't you understand how dangerous these drugs are?'

I saw all my precious Mandrax and Durophet scattered about on the bathroom floor and I lost my temper.

'Call a cab!' I yelled back at him. 'I'm leaving! You have no business going through my bags! Who the hell do you think you are?'

I was naked, but I didn't care as I got up and faced him with my hands on my hips. If Brian hadn't been as upset as he was, he'd probably have laughed at me.

'I don't use the pills the way you think,' I said with a steely edge to my voice. 'My drugs are my business and you have no right to throw them on the floor and yell at me. They're mine, and mine alone.'

Brian was still upset, but he tried to calm me down, explaining that he was worried about me. I didn't listen. I packed a small suitcase and took the train to London the same day.

I don't know what Brian did with my tablets, but I'm quite sure he flushed them down the toilet.

When I got to London, my friends were happy to see me. I stayed for a couple of days and enjoyed myself. I went to the clubs and restaurants and did some shopping. My friends and acquaintances asked me where I'd been and I told them that I'd moved to the country and was living with a man. I didn't tell them it was Brian.

After visiting my doctor in Harley Street, two days after my return to London and with new prescriptions for Durophet and Mandrax in my hand, my anger slowly vanished and I longed for home and Brian. I hadn't felt this kind of longing since I was a little girl living with my parents. I ached for Brian and I was willing to forgive him for being so heavy-handed about my drugs. In my heart, I know his anger was well-founded. He loved me and cared for me and he didn't want me to become a drug addict.

I took the first train back and Brian was overjoyed when I returned. Our reconciliation made me happy, too, and I felt at one with the world again.

During my stay in London, Brian had started to worry about my parents in Stockholm. Maybe it was because he had found my tablets. I don't know why, but he insisted I should call my parents and tell them who I was living with.

'You're their only daughter,' he said. 'Imagine if we had a daughter and she went abroad without ringing or sending a word about her whereabouts. I'd go crazy — I wouldn't be able to sleep! Please, call your mother now!'

Brian handed me the receiver and dialled the number. I talked to my mother and told her I was all right, but I didn't tell her about Brian. I just told her that I'd met a man, fallen in love and moved in with him.

Brian didn't mention my tablets again. He was happy I was

back and I guess he didn't want to dampen the high spirits. I forgave Brian and realised that I couldn't blame him. He'd witnessed a lot of misery surrounding drug abuse, and had experienced the repercussions. My conscience got the better of me and I decided to reduce my intake of both Mandrax and Durophet.

A few weeks later, I made a huge mistake. I'd woken up before Brian and, as usual, had gone down to the kitchen to prepare his breakfast. For some reason, I felt a bit bored and sneaked up the stairs again and swallowed a Mandrax. Since I'd reduced my intake of the drug I spaced out, and when I came round, Brian went crazy. I was giggly and gave him a silly smile without seeing the anger in his eyes The whole thing ended with Brian dragging me to the bathroom where he held my head under the shower until I sobered up.

The incident made me stop taking Mandrax and Durophet — for Brian's sake.

CHAPTER TEN

THE
STONES

BRIAN

I didn't meet any of the other members of the Rolling Stones while I was living with Brian. He told me that there had been problems with the band and that nothing had been the same since Anita left him for Keith — or, as he put it, since Keith took Anita from him.

Brian often pointed out that the Rolling Stones had been his band. He was the one who'd started the band and named it, and he wanted them to go on playing the music which had made them famous.

'In the beginning, we all had the same aim,' Brian said. 'The only thing we wanted was to play the music we could all stand by and I was the driving force.'

Brian was the one who had created that special Stones sound, the 'dirty' sound, and he'd experimented on different instruments to produce it.

'I know Mick wanted to be the frontman,' Brian said, 'And I

didn't mind as long as it didn't interfere with our music.'

Brian never wanted to be Mick. As he saw it, the rivalry between him and Mick was due to the fact that Brian and Keith enjoyed playing together and could spend hours doing just that. Mick may have felt left out since he couldn't play any instruments.

When Mick and Keith eventually started writing songs, they never asked Brian to join them. And, as a result, the new relationship between Mick and Keith made Brian feel like an outsider. He told me that, on several occasions, he'd tried to introduce a new sound or a new instrument, but Mick and Keith had turned him down. Their lack of interest had hurt him deeply. He began to feel frozen out and lonely, and not only musically.

It is wrong to say that Brian didn't like Mick — he loved Mick and he liked Keith. He admired them for writing such good music. The only thing that nagged him was that he wished they'd let him be more involved in creating the songs. But at the same time, he understood that his contribution to the band was his ability to play different instruments and finding new, exciting sounds for their music.

'When we started out, our primary aim was to reach out with our music and make a name for ourselves,' Brian said. 'But when we attracted attention we started getting other problems.

'We had much less to do with one another. The money began to control our lives, as much as the music, or our friendship. Everything came down to making money. We weren't a band any more', Brian concluded, 'it seemed to me as if we were a money-making machine.'

While I lived with Brian, the Stones were recording 'Honky Tonk Women', which was finished the day after Brian's funeral.

*   *   *

Brian's decision to leave the Stones began to form one afternoon when someone from the studio called and told Brian that a car would pick him up between nine and ten the following morning.

Later that evening, Brian was really on edge and told me he didn't want to go to the studio. He slept badly and when the morning came, he was a mess. He woke up earlier than usual and started to prod me gently.

'Anna ... Anna, are you awake?' he whispered. 'Please, will you do me a favour?'

I knew intuitively what Brian wanted. He was hoping to persuade me to go down to the driver and tell him that Brian was ill and that he couldn't go to the studio.

Reluctantly, I agreed to talk to him.

The pattern was repeated over the next couple of days. After three or four days, I told Brian I'd had enough. I didn't want to lie any more and I felt sorry for the driver, who'd had to drive to Cotchford Farm and then back to London every day. I pulled the duvet over my head and pretended to sleep, blocking out Brian's pleas. I said that he was a coward and that it was his duty to see the driver himself.

But Brian was extremely stubborn and tried to persuade me otherwise. I tried to make him understand that I didn't want to be involved and explained that I'd probably be accused of being the reason for his absence.

'You're such a coward!' I came out with. 'It's not my duty to run your errands!'

'I'll go down tomorrow,' Brian said. 'I promise. Please, Anna, just this once? Please ...'

Finally, I couldn't stand his nagging. Annoyed, I went down to the driver with another ridiculous excuse. He left and gave the message to the others at the studio.

Time passed, and after a while the other band members were fed up with Brian's behaviour — and I didn't blame them.

'I *will* settle this,' Brian said. 'I'm going to talk to them. I promise.'

I found the whole situation really awkward. Everybody but the journalists knew that Brian had a new girlfriend and I felt that they blamed me for Brian's absence. I tried to make him go to London to talk to the others. I explained that I could understand why they thought he just didn't care and I also reminded him that they were a band and they were recording a new song. If he was a member of that band, then he should take part in the recording.

Brian refused to listen. It didn't matter what I said. He acted like a little boy bunking off school. He felt guilty, but at the same time he was relieved to get out of the studio work.

*   *   *

One night, we sat down in the kitchen to talk. Brian said that he'd made up his mind. He wanted to leave the Rolling Stones. At first, I thought I'd misunderstood him. When my initial surprise had passed, I looked inquiringly at him.

'Are you sure that's what you really want?' I asked him. 'Think it over carefully. You might enjoy your life in the country right now, but who knows what will happen in a few months' time? You might change your mind and start missing the life you have with the Stones.'

Brian explained to me that the Stones no longer played the kind of music he could identify with. Their musical taste had moved on. He felt he had his roots in rhythm 'n' blues, and that was the kind of music he wanted to play. The others didn't share his taste, having gone their own way.

'It's not only the music,' Brian said. 'I can't face working with Keith any more. It'll never be the same again.'

Brian said that he realised his relationship with Anita was

destructive, but I'm sure he was more hurt than he wanted to admit when he heard that Keith and Anita were expecting their first child.

But the only thing he said about Anita was that he feared that she would be disastrous for Keith.

'I'm sure she'll drag him down into drugs, the way she dragged me down,' Brian said. 'She can't live without drugs, they're essential to her world.'

'It's easy for you to blame Anita,' I replied. 'She's not here to defend herself. It might well have been that she was more experienced than you and experimented more. But you can't blame Anita for your problems. You were old enough to make your own decisions when you met her, right? You can hardly accuse her of seducing an inexperienced schoolboy.'

Brian refused to listen. He could be quite stubborn and he continued to blame Anita for most of his problems with drugs.

'I'm lucky she's gone,' he said. 'The drugs controlled my life for years. They're only an escape from reality and I'll never end up in that swamp again.'

I believed him. He meant what he said. But it wasn't the whole truth. His extreme views against drugs sprang directly from the two occasions when he'd been busted.

'I'll never forget the fright I had when the coppers rushed into my flat,' Brian said. 'I thought they were going to kill me. It was terrible.'

Brian was too soft to handle confrontations with tough guys. The mere thought of the police and the courts terrified him.

'I'm really happy that I'm off the drugs and away from all the misery,' Brian said. 'But I know that I'm still vulnerable. I might end up on drugs again if I move in those circles.'

The Stones did. And Brian knew it.

*   *   *

Brian had conflicting feelings towards the Stones. He wanted to leave the band, but he was afraid of doing so. He really wanted to take a break from the Stones to consider the future and his role in the band. But a long American tour lay ahead and Brian didn't want to go. It was rumoured later that Brian had been refused a visa to the US because of his drug record. But Mick and Keith had both been fined for drug offences and so I can't understand why Brian would have been singled out.

Brian never mentioned the visa. He was more concerned about his lack of options. He had to come to a decision, and fast.

Today, it's easier for me to understand Brian's dilemma. Breaking up with the Stones was probably similar to ending a marriage; even if the relationship has become unbearable, it's still difficult to do.

Brian was never disparaging when he talked about the other members of the Stones.

'We've known each other for years,' he said. 'You can't dislike a person because he doesn't share your views.'

Mick Jagger was the only one who upset Brian now and then. According to Brian, Mick always tried to promote himself as the only member of the band who dissociated himself from drugs.

'But he never says no when he's offered!' Brian exclaimed. 'He never admits to doing anything wrong ... but he's always ready to judge other people — except for Keith, that is. He needs him because they complement each other and Mick can't write the music without Keith.'

During this time, we had long, tortuous conversations about the pros and cons of Brian leaving the Stones. I couldn't advise him. It was a decision he had to make himself and that made him frustrated.

Brian was happy just pottering about on the farm. It had become his life. He loved waking up to a day without demands. He enjoyed his new life.

But when he talked about the Stones, I saw pain in his eyes, and it saddened me.

I personally didn't care about the Rolling Stones. I was in love with Brian, but I understood his dilemma. Brian loved the Stones, had known them for years, lived with them, been on tour with them and enjoyed their company. The Stones had been a part of his life for a long time and the band also represented a secure income.

One evening, we sat at the kitchen table opposite each other. Brian swept away his hair from his eyes, reached across and took my hand.

'I think it'll be okay, Anna. They'll manage without me.'

'I'm sure they will,' I replied. 'But will you manage without them?'

Brian didn't answer. He stood up and disappeared from the kitchen. A while later, he returned with his guitar. I can still see him in my mind's eye. His blond hair, the fringe almost hiding his eyes. He sat down on his favourite chair and leaned back. He closed his eyes and he started to play.

When the chord lazily became a tune he looked at me with a big smile and my heart warmed. I felt sure that he'd manage splendidly without the Stones. He was a fabulous, talented musician and had a unique feeling about music.

Brian had the talent to be able to produce a kind of music in which old and new were mixed in his own brilliant way. I felt sure that his name would be huge in the music business even without the Stones. It's tragic that we were deprived of his remarkable talent.

'I want to start a new band and have the feeling I had with the Stones at the beginning of our career,' Brian said when he put down his guitar.

'I want to be able to play the kind of music I believe in and be appreciated for it. It was an incredible feeling when things started to happen with the Stones, when people began to listen to our music and told us they liked it. My dearest wish is to revive that feeling again.'

Fame was another matter. Brian said that he didn't mind if he had to go without it. At least, the negative aspects which came with fame: The hangers-on, the false friends, the bodyguards, the police and the trials.

*   *   *

Brian was backed into a corner. He had to make a decision about the Rolling Stones. He was in two minds. He wanted to quit, but couldn't bring himself to make the move. He had long talks with John Lennon, who supported him. I'm sure that John said that he'd left the Beatles, but maybe it wasn't made official until the following year.

On some days, Brian called John three or four times. John encouraged Brian and told him that he would be fine without the Stones.

'You can't lie to yourself,' John said to Brian. 'Whatever happens, you're the only one that matters. If you lose the unique talent, you have nothing left, and you can never replace it.

'You may grieve for a while, and you may be depressed. But remember one thing; money can't, and won't, rule our lives. We should be ruled by our creativity.'

John was unequivocal and Brian listened to him. He knew that money had begun to rule his life the day he bought Cotchford Farm and he was worried about a future without the money the Stones brought him. And he was no longer on his own; he was responsible for other people as well, such as Mrs Hallett and Mick Martin.

Brian knew in his heart that John was right. But Brian still had to convince himself that he was doing the right thing.

John's unwavering support made Brian think about a new band.

'I don't want any famous musicians in the band,' he said. 'The important thing is that they have the right feeling for the music I want to play.'

I know Brian discussed the matter with Alexis Korner, who also encouraged him and was a great support.

Brian hated any sort of conflict and he detested rows. Instead of doing the sensible thing and telling the other members of the Stones that he wanted to quit, he forced a separation by refusing to go to the studio. But when the others got in touch with him and told him that he was out, he was still shocked. The decision to leave the Stones had been taken away from him. Instead, Mick, Keith, Bill and Charlie asked him to quit. Brian had no appeal. He agreed to leave the band and they decided to meet to draft a statement for the press.

The meeting with the Stones was preceded by long calls to John, who cheered Brian up and made him think of his future career. He bolstered Brian's self-esteem by telling him that the Stones needed him more than he needed them.

John was a great friend to Brian. He even took time to come down to Cotchford Farm and give him moral support. They spent a couple of hours in the music room playing together, and I didn't want to disturb them. I know that Brian needed to be alone with John. I was in the garden reading when John came out to say goodbye.

'Take care of Brian,' he said. 'He needs you now. He'll do all right without the Stones, but he needs your help in the beginning. Try to support him and cheer him up.'

Both Brian and I were grateful to John for the support he gave us. It meant a lot, especially to Brian.

*   *   *

Brian was agitated and uneasy before the meeting with the other members of the Stones. He woke early and started to wander about the house, asking me to follow him. He wouldn't let me out of his sight. After a while, I tired of walking around and decided to go up to the bedroom, lie down on the bed and read a book. I wasn't alone for more than a minute or two before Brian came up and lay down next to me.

He started to caress me and I put the book down. I knew his career was to take a new path that day and I could feel his nervousness. We made love, slowly and tenderly and some of Brian's tension was eased.

We lay silently in the bed with our arms around one another and Emily jumped up and lay down at my feet. It was a peaceful moment, but it was interrupted when we heard a car coming down the private road, stopping in the courtyard.

Brian quietly got out of bed and threw his clothes on, just as I heard people getting out of the car. One of the car doors was shut with an almighty thud. I got up and walked towards the window.

In the courtyard, I saw Mick's white Mercedes. 'What kind of car do you want?' he asked me again. 'I was thinking of buying a new Rolls Royce, but what for? What do you want? A Mercedes?'

'It can wait,' I said. 'You'd better get down there and open the door. You can't leave them waiting.'

I saw Mick, Keith and Charlie, but not Bill. They had all stepped out of the car and were on their way to the front door. Brian gave me a kiss and ran down the stairs.

I went back to bed. Something stopped me from going downstairs. I felt I had nothing to do down there. It was as if a relationship, a love affair, was over and I felt that the parting had to be done in the gentlest way possible.

I could hear Brian showing them into the dining room and I wondered why Bill wasn't with them. Maybe he thought it would be ugly. He was right. I couldn't make out the voices, but there was plenty of talk and indiscriminate shouting. Strangely enough, it was Brian who seemed to be the more controlled. He'd prepared for this moment for a long time, even though he'd never thought the final decision would come so quickly.

The hubbub died down and, after a while, Mick, Keith and Charlie left the house. I heard the car doors slam and the Mercedes start up, and shortly afterwards the three of them were on their way back to London — one member less.

I stood at the window and watched the car disappear uphill in a cloud of dust, then I went back to bed. I was worried about Brian, but I didn't want to disturb him. Maybe he needed to be alone for a while.

I didn't have to wait long. After a couple of minutes, I heard Brian's light footsteps on the stairs.

'It's over,' he said when he came through the door. 'We're still friends and we respect each other. We promised to co-operate in one way or another. Help and support each other.

'I don't have to worry about money either,' he added. 'I'll get what I'm entitled to.'

Then Brian held out a small packet towards me, and smiled.

'Keith brought me a present, as a good mate. He wanted me to have a pleasant evening.'

The packet contained cocaine. I'm not sure I would have called it a present from a 'good' friend. It was definitely an ill-advised gesture of friendship. But Brian was pleased. Keith had thought about him and that made him happy.

By the evening, Brian had made the most of the cocaine. He was flying through the house, and his misery continued into the night. I had to help him to the toilet where he threw up several times. I'd never seen Brian in this state before and I was scared that he wouldn't wake up if he fell asleep. And I didn't dare call his doctor, either. I knew why Brian was feeling bad, but I

149

couldn't tell anyone. Instead, I dragged him around the house until dawn, when I decided that he'd come round enough to go to bed.

In my mind, I cursed Keith and his 'present'. It was a lot easier to understand Brian's actions. The separation had been hard on him and the cocaine was an escape. The main problem was that Brian hadn't taken any drugs for months, maybe years. The cocaine was too strong for him, and his body couldn't cope. It objected — loudly.

*   *   *

The day after the meeting, on the 8 June 1969, the newspapers printed stories about Brian leaving the Stones and Cotchford Farm was besieged by the press. Until then, I hadn't really understood just how famous the Stones actually were. Maybe it was because Brian and I had lived a quiet and protected life over the last few months without being bothered by journalists or photographers.

Brian refused to be interviewed. He had made his statement, and that was enough. Brian wasn't his usual happy self when he woke up that particular morning following the split. He found it hard to get out of bed. He was still reeling from the cocaine trip, but he was also relieved that his break with the Stones was definite.

'I don't regret it,' he said. 'It took a long time to get this far and now it only feels like a relief.'

During the day, the telephone rang continuously. I think every member of the Stones talked with Brian to ask how he was, and many other friends and acquaintances called as well.

One of the first to ring was John Lennon. He said he thought Brian had been strong to take the step and had done what he felt was the best for him.

'Don't give in!' were his final words.

I spent most of the day by the pool. I swam, lay in the sun and enjoyed the warm weather. In the afternoon, Brian left the house and came wandering out into the garden. He was restless and thoughtful.

'If the photographers take pictures of you they'll think it's me,' he said and gave my black bikini bottoms a knowing look.

I seldom used the top and with my short, blonde hair the photographers, if they were at a distance, could easily mistake me for Brian.

Brian often said that I was provocative, but at the same time he assured me that he didn't want me to change.

'I love you the way you are,' he often pointed out. 'And I want you to be with me always.'

The split from the Stones was heart-rending for several reasons. It wasn't only the fact that Brian had parted from Mick, Keith, Bill and Charlie, with whom he'd been 'living' for so long. He was also worried about how people in general were going to react, particularly if they thought that he'd let both them and the Stones down.

'What am I going to say in defence of my quitting the Stones?' he asked me several times during the day. 'How can I make them understand?'

He knew that the journalists wouldn't help him.

'They're my worst enemies,' Brian grumbled. 'They just love to write scandal about me. They're probably having a field day today.'

Reluctantly, he admitted that he'd gladly contributed to messy headlines at the start of his career. He also said that his set phrase in those days had been, 'I need to read the paper today, to find out what I was up to yesterday!'

However, when I met him, he was tired of playing the decadent rock star. He wanted to be able to reach out to people and make them understand that he'd changed his lifestyle, but he didn't know how to do it.

'It'll come out all right,' I said. 'Give them time. You just have to keep living the way you do now and even the journalists will eventually realise that you're not the same old Brian you used to be.'

The days following his break-up with the Stones, Brian lurched between joy and despair. I had to look after him more than usual and we talked through the nights. But even if Brian was feeling sad about everything that had happened, he looked to the future with hope and confidence and, instead of grieving over what had been, we began to make plans for the future.

CHAPTER ELEVEN

THE
FUTURE

BRIAN

A few days after his split from the Stones, Brian was back to his normal self again, happy and content with his life. He was playing with Luther in the garden when he suddenly looked up at me and asked if I wanted to add a couple of cocker spaniel puppies to our little family.

Cocker spaniels had been my favourite breed since childhood, and every birthday and Christmas a puppy was at the top of my wish list. Now my dreams would come true. I was going to have a house filled with cocker spaniels!

'Yes! Oh, yes!' I exclaimed, and threw myself into Brian's arms. He laughed at me and whirled me round in the air.

Later that day, he got in touch with the breeder who'd been responsible for Luther, and after talking to her for a while he ordered three cocker spaniel puppies, one black, one yellow and one red. Brian said he'd send Joan to pick up the puppies. While we were waiting, we arranged a playpen in the kitchen to stop them from running around before they were house-trained.

When we were finished, Brian and I looked at each other and laughed.

'We're probably out of our minds, both of us,' I said.

But we loved animals and we had room for more than two dogs and a cat, who never wanted to be cuddled and lived an independent life. I only saw him eating in the kitchen from time to time and then he'd disappear again. He didn't even have a name, and I think he moved into the house without an invitation, or maybe he was there when Brian bought the house, and stayed on.

We also talked about buying a couple of horses, and maybe hens, but it wasn't to be.

The puppies were lovely and so excitable there wasn't a dull moment after their arrival. Brian gave me one of the puppies. I chose the red one and called her Lolita. The other bitch was given the name Baby Jane, and the third, the black male, we called Boy.

Emily didn't like the puppies. She was probably jealous, and she made me aware of her feelings as soon as I cuddled one of the puppies. Luther, on the other hand, loved them and appointed himself stepfather. He slept outside the playpen to keep an eye on them and he happily allowed them to pull on his ears and tail. But he also knew where to draw the line and made sure they behaved themselves when they were going too far.

When the puppies were playing on the lawn, we couldn't help but laugh at them. They were three little rascals with a huge amount of energy and even Luther was exhausted from time to time trying to keep up with them.

With the puppies in the house, we were forced to get out of bed early in the morning to feed them and clean the playpen. The three of them were so happy to see us and ran over with tails wagging when we came into the room.

Since it was Brian's idea to buy the puppies, I used to wake him up and remind him that it was time to go down to the kitchen and feed them. He always tried to wriggle out of helping me, but now and then I succeeded in persuading him to make himself useful.

The puppies brought joy to the house and their energy was catching. Brian spent hours in the music room and he invited different musicians to the house to test them. I never met them as I didn't want to interfere. The lovely summer weather continued and I spent most of my days in the garden, by the pool.

It was around this time that Brian talked to John Lennon and Alexis Korner about the new band he was going to put together.

'It's important to me to get on with the work properly,' Brian said to me. 'I want to put this new band together as fast as I can. I'm sure it'll be great if I work with the right people.'

On the whole, Brian was cheerful and optimistic after his break-up with the Stones. You could tell by his behaviour that he was happy and relaxed. And he brought up the subject of marriage more often than before.

One day, when Frank, Brian and I were sitting in the dining room, Brian reached for a napkin and wrote something on it. When he'd finished, he asked Frank to witness his signature. Frank did so, and Brian smiled at me and gave me the napkin. My heart warmed when I saw what he'd written on it and I blushed as I read:

Anna, will you marry me?
Brian Jones

In the presence of:
Frank Thorogood

I felt embarrassed and instead of saying 'Yes, I will,' which I wanted to do, I laughed and tore the napkin to pieces. It's something I have regretted ever since.

When we'd gone to bed the same evening, Brian turned over to me.

'I guess you're the kind of girl who wants to be engaged for a couple of years before you get married?' he said teasingly.

'Maybe I am,' I teased back.

*   *   *

The following day, Brian decided to invite some friends down for the forthcoming weekend. He said it was about time we had a social life and met some people other than Frank, Mrs Hallett and Mick Martin.

We had a lovely time and Brian's friends let me know that they'd never seen Brian looking so content. They felt that I was the right girl for him, that we complemented each other. I think we did. We shared a mutual respect and we were never unkind to each other. I listened to him and he was always interested in my opinion. My feelings carried great weight. I was the one he talked to when he was thinking about something, and he was the one I turned to for the same reason.

When we first met, I thought that Brian and I would have a short love affair. I'd had boyfriends in the past, but my feelings towards them were never serious. And when one or two had proposed, I didn't know what to do — so I ran away. My opinion was that I was too young and, as I saw it, my life had just begun. But after the first month with Brian, I realised that the feelings I had towards him were serious.

Brian constantly worried about my age. He was afraid that I was not ready to make a commitment. But on the other hand, he wanted to get married and have children, and I was the one he wanted to marry. Brian was old-fashioned when it came to marriage and he asked me if we could go to Sweden to meet my parents.

'I want to ask your father for your hand,' he said. 'I want to see your parents and tell them that I'll take care of you.

'Do you think they'll like me? I know all about the Rolling Stones' reputation, but they might accept me now when they know I've left the band. Maybe they could come over here and meet my parents? It'd give them a chance to find out who I am. Do you think they'd like that?'

Brian was always worrying about not being good enough, and he was considerate and generous.

When he was worried, my heart melted and I loved to sweep away his fringe and look at his beautiful face, a face that few have seen. A beautiful face.

Brian used to joke around when we'd taken a bath and would comb his hair up, making it stand on end. But his hair was too long and it soon fell back into place.

He looked different without his hair covering most of his face. But he was good-looking with or without his long, sweeping hair. His face was one of the most beautiful I have ever seen.

*   *   *

One day, Shirley Arnold from the Stones' office called and asked for Brian. I passed the phone to Brian and they talked for a while. I went back out into the garden and Brian soon followed me. He told me that Shirley had asked if it was all right if a girl called Helen Spittal came down to Cotchford Farm to see him.

Brian explained that Helen was one of his oldest and most faithful fans whom he hadn't seen for quite some time. He told me that she would like to come down to visit the following day.

Brian said that he'd take the opportunity to tell her why he left the Stones and that he was planning a new band.

He was restless before Helen's arrival and asked me what he should do to entertain her.

I admit that I was a bit jealous when Brian talked about Helen. I didn't understand why she was coming down to see him at all.

When Helen arrived, Brian introduced us, but since Helen came to see Brian I left them and went out into the garden while Brian showed her the house and told her about his new life and his plans for the future.

After a while, Brian took Helen for a walk in the garden and then they came and sat down next to me. Helen and I talked about the Stones and the forthcoming concert at Hyde Park. She said she was planning to go and see them and Brian and I told her that we'd probably see her there.

Helen was a nice girl and I realised that Brian needn't have worried about her visit. He had no problem entertaining Helen. She was probably just happy that he'd agreed to see her.

The following weekend, John Mayall, his wife Pamela and their children came down to visit us. John was a musician whom Brian really admired. He was called 'the father of the British blues movement' and had founded John Mayall's Bluesbreakers in 1963.

It wasn't long before Brian and John ended up in the music room where they played together for a couple of hours. I sat down and listened to them for a while. I enjoyed listening to Brian playing. He fascinated me and also made me a bit envious since he'd mastered most instruments.

John was fun and good company, and so were the children, but Pamela seemed a bit stand-offish right from the start.

'We've been to the French Riviera,' she said snobbily. 'Where have you been for your holiday?'

'Here,' I said. 'You can get a good tan here as well.'

When I moved in with Brian he teased me and called me his 'little asparagus', but the beautiful weather and the sunny days had made a difference. My tan was even deeper than Pamela's, in spite of her luxurious break.

Pamela didn't approve of my cheek, and dismissed me with a frown. I didn't like her. She talked too much. Among other things, she gossiped about Marianne Faithfull, who was supposed to have been one of her best friends. She talked about Marianne's experiences with drugs and other personal matters. To make my feelings known, I went for a walk with the dogs.

After a while, Brian came running after me.

'Good girl!' he laughed. 'Tell her off, by all means!'

We sneaked away to our special place, the arbour, and made love without any consideration for our guests; my good temper returned.

When we got back, Pamela asked me how I could stand living in the country.

'It's a question of taste and who you're living with,' I said.

With the exception of Pamela's behaviour, we had a beautiful day. Brian amused the children in the swimming pool where he entertained them with his skills. I remember that he leapt from the springboard and dived into the water pretending to be different animals. The children collapsed with laughter and Brian enjoyed the attention.

When the children finally left the pool, he told them to take off their wet swimming things.

'There are some dry clothes over there,' he said pointing at the clothes line. 'Help yourselves!'

The only 'clothes' hanging on the line were bits of my underwear. Brian teased me for having a large number of different panties and bras, and eventually I stopped wearing any underwear at all. It made things easier when we went for a walk and felt the desire to make love.

When the children had run off, Brian hugged me and giggled like a teenager. He enjoyed teasing the children as much as the adults.

The following weekend, Alexis Korner and his wife Bobbie came down to visit us. They were Brian's oldest and closest friends.

'Alexis and Bobbie took care of me when I first came to London,' he said. 'They gave me food and a roof over my head. And they encouraged me to keep on playing. I owe them everything.'

The day before their arrival, Brian told me that Bobbie was the most beautiful woman in the world. He said I would understand what he meant when I met her.

Brian was right. Bobbie was a sweet and beautiful woman with long, black hair, almond-shaped brown eyes and classical features. Alexis was as handsome as his wife was beautiful, with his thick, curly hair. I still consider them the nicest people I have ever met and you could tell that they loved and respected each other, and everyone else who was in their circle.

Brian was calm and relaxed in Alexis and Bobbie's company and after their first visit he said that he wished he could have the same luck in love as them.

'I want a marriage that lasts for ever,' he said, 'exactly like Alexis and Bobbie. They've been married for nineteen years! Imagine that! Nineteen years!'

When I close my eyes, I can see Bobbie in my mind. Her beauty, her calmness — and her nasty-smelling cigarillos! Bobbie never smoked hashish like Alexis, but Alexis respected Brian's feelings when it came to drugs and he was tactful.

On the very first occasion I met Alexis, we sneaked onto the garden together and shared a joint, and we continued to sneak out like two kids whenever he came to visit. We had our own code when Alexis wanted me to join him.

'Anna!' he said. 'I want you to show me your garden.'

Then we called for the dogs and told Brian and Bobbie that we were going for a walk. As soon as we were away from the house, Alexis would light a joint and we'd laugh and think ourselves terribly clever. But I suspect that Brian knew what was going on.

Whenever Alexis and Bobbie came down to visit us, Brian was overjoyed, although he still felt guilty about not being in touch with them during his years with the Stones.

'I was so self-centred that I forgot about them,' he said. 'It wasn't until I started to think about what's important in life that I remembered Alexis and his wonderful family. Now I want to do whatever I can to make it up to them and return some of the respect, friendship and love they gave me when I needed it most.'

On one occasion, Brian insisted that I should treat the Korners to a typical Swedish meal. He remembered the Swedish meat balls he'd enjoyed when he was in Sweden with the Stones and asked me to call my mother and get the recipe.

Bobbie and Alexis had three children and I was rolling meat balls for a whole day to make enough for seven people. And I peeled 6lb of potatoes to make mashed potatoes. My mother had given me a can of red whortleberry which I served with the meal.

The meat balls were a huge success and when we were finished there was nothing left. Brian smiled proudly at me and I promised to make meat balls for him whenever he wanted.

Brian's guilt over Alexis and Bobbie surfaced now and then when they visited us. He wanted to give them the moon and the stars and constantly asked if there was anything he could do for them. Alexis and Bobbie hugged him and said that he needn't worry. The main thing was that they had found each other again.

Brian felt it was of the utmost importance that people liked him. He loved to hear me say nice things about him when I spoke to my friends. He would even ask me to tell them about our everyday life, that he'd repaired my shoe, forced me to drink full-fat milk, hugged me a thousand times and picked flowers for me. He wanted to be a part of my life and he wanted my friends to know he loved and took good care of me.

When I talked to my parents, he often sat next to me listening. He didn't understand Swedish, but he wanted me to translate our conversations.

'Tell them about all the filthy things I've done with their daughter and they'll force me to marry you!' he teased.

Brian continued to talk about marriage and said that he wanted a family to take care of and to come home to. He talked about his sons and said that he wished they would come and live with him, and he dreamt about becoming a dad again.

'I'm longing for the day when someone crawls up into the bed and wakes me up early in the morning and says, "Dad! Dad! Wake up! I want to show you something!" just like I did when I was a kid.'

Brian often talked about his father and told me that he had always been there for him and had tried to understand him. He loved his father and deeply regretted that he'd hurt him during his wild years. But he promised to turn over a new leaf and he felt that they were finding the way back to each other.

I lived with Brian round the clock and he had many ideas. There was always something new he wanted to try. He planned and talked about the future and you never could tell his next move. He was impulsive and unpredictable. That was one of the reasons why I didn't take Brian's talk about marriage and children too seriously.

I had always wanted a big family with lots of children and animals, and even though I was young I knew it was a huge responsibility. I wanted to make sure that Brian had meant what he said, and I didn't want either marriage or children to be just another whim.

But it was impossible to bring Brian to a stand-still when he'd made up his mind and he soon gave me further evidence of his stubbornness.

* * *

It was a hot, sunny day and I'd just slipped into the pool when Brian came running from the house with a T-shirt in his hand.

'Put this on and follow me!' he said excitedly. 'I want to show you something!'

He took my hand and ran towards the house, leading me inside and up the stairs to the first floor, dragging me into the 'nursery'. The room was empty except for a couple of tins of paint. Brian proudly showed me the paint he'd mixed himself, producing a colour he called 'Moroccan blue'. The walls in the room were white and Brian dipped a brush into one of the tins, and proceeded to apply a wide blue stroke to the wall.

'What do you think? Nice, isn't it?'

He looked at me proudly and his eyes sparkled.

'This is for Johanna!'

'Who?' I asked, taken aback.

'Our daughter,' Brian said. 'I want her to have the name Johanna. This is going to be her room. I want her to see this beautiful blue colour when she wakes up in the morning.

'By the way, I've decided to make her a bed myself,' he added and looked even prouder.

'Pick up a brush,' he ordered. 'Let's paint and dream.'

The colour was nice when the rays of sunshine fell across it and Brian was as happy as a lark. I wasn't prepared to be a mother quite yet, but Brian was overjoyed and I didn't have the heart to start an argument with him.

I picked up a brush and started to paint. When we'd finished the first of the four walls it was late in the afternoon. Brian took my hand and we sat on the floor to admire our 'Moroccan' handiwork.

'You will be a perfect mum,' he said. 'Johanna will have your eyes and nose and my mouth and hair.'

Brian kept on dreaming about his daughter. 'You'll have to teach her Swedish,' he said. 'It's an advantage to speak two languages.'

He hugged me and looked deep into my eyes.

'For the first time I know I'm going to be a good father,' he said. 'And I hope our first child will be a little girl.'

I can still see him in my mind talking about our 'daughter'. It was nice and safe sitting on the floor in the 'nursery' with Brian's arms around me; my love for him was almost tangible. Brian was one happy smile and it was easy to get carried away. In the loving surroundings, a thought began to grow. Maybe it was time to be a mother. Maybe it was meant to be.

Later that evening, Brian smiled as he emptied my pills down the toilet and flushed them away.

I remember waking up in the middle of the night and looking at Brian, who was sleeping on his stomach with his face turned towards me. He held my hand in a firm grip and even in his sleep he looked pleased. When he was in this positive frame of mind, my heart ached with love. He made me incredibly happy, and even if I hadn't planned to start a family just yet, he gave me hope for the future and the thought of becoming a mother didn't scare me any more.

I thought about our first child and wondered what she'd look like. The only thing I knew for sure was that she would probably be short. Brian wasn't tall and neither was I, and our child would definitely not be a giant. Her hair could be either blonde or dark and she would probably have blue or greyish-blue eyes. But it wasn't important; the main thing was that she was healthy.

I smiled when I looked at Brian and I felt my love for him deepen. And I remember my last thought before I fell asleep again. Whoever the little girl resembled, I was sure that our child would have a father and a mother who loved her deeply.

CHAPTER TWELVE

THE
BEAM

B rian's disapproval of Frank and the work that he'd done on the house reached its climax on the Sunday evening before Brian's death.

Brian and I were alone at Cotchford Farm and we'd just finished dinner when the telephone rang. I went to the kitchen to answer it. It was a friend of mine, Jan Olsson, who worked in the music business and had been living in London for some time. He called to invite Brian and me to his forthcoming wedding and I accepted immediately. We chatted for a while in Swedish.

Brian cleared the table and followed me into the kitchen. He didn't understand what Jan and I were talking about and I could tell by his facial expression that he was getting a bit annoyed. He started circling around me, frowning and I soon realised that his jealousy was growing by the minute.

Suddenly, he pushed me to the floor.

'What the hell are you doing?' I shouted at him, convinced

that he'd had another attack of jealousy.

In the fall, I dropped the receiver and the next second one of the support beams in the ceiling collapsed with a loud crash. It landed an inch from my head.

If Brian hadn't pushed me away, the heavy beam would have fallen directly onto my head and I would probably have died. When I realised what had happened, I started to tremble. Brian was as shocked as me, and he kneeled down and tried to comfort me.

After a while, we got up and looked at the beam. One end rested on the table, the other on the floor. Brian told me to leave the kitchen while he took a look at the remaining beams to check that they were safe.

He then came into the dining room and sat down next to me.

'You could have been killed!' he said. 'I knew I couldn't trust Frank and this time he's gone too far. I'm going to call Fred and tell him to stop Frank's payments. He's not getting another penny from me!'

I was still in shock when Brian went to the telephone to get Fred's home number from Les Perrin. I could hear that he was upset, but I didn't hear what he said.

Brian returned after a while. He'd talked to Fred and felt a lot better.

'Frank is going to pay for this,' he said. 'The fucking bastard is responsible for his workmen and since he's approved their work he is directly to blame, and I'm not going to let him get away with it.

'You could have died,' Brian repeated angrily. 'I would never have forgiven myself if you did. I'm paying Frank to work, not to socialise with him,' he continued. 'It's my own doing, but enough is enough. I won't have anything to do with him again!'

I agreed. The mistake Frank had made was lethal. I could have been killed. Or Mrs Hallett. Or Brian. Or even Frank. I understood Brian's anger and I was still shaken about what had happened.

'I don't need Frank,' Brian continued. 'I can contact one of the other builders I've talked to and let them finish the work on the house. The only reason I hired Frank was because he'd worked at Keith's. I've got no obligation towards him.'

I was pleased that, at long last, Brian had decided to get rid of Frank. I didn't like having him around. He wasn't good company for Brian, and I hadn't trusted him for ages. I had tried to talk to Brian about my suspicions, but he wouldn't listen. He merely thought that I was jealous of his relationship with Frank.

'I think I know now what you've been trying to tell me,' Brian said after a while. 'You never trusted Frank from the start, right?'

'Right, and I meant every word,' I said. 'I've been trying to make you see that Frank is no good for you. He isn't doing a proper job and he isn't a friend of yours. The only interest he has in you is your money — and maybe your status.

'It's time that you stand up for yourself and tell him what you really think. You've got nothing to worry about. Ask him to leave, once and for all!'

'I told Fred to see to it that I get copies of Frank's bills first thing in the morning,' Brian said. 'And I told him not to pay a penny more before I've had time to look through them.'

Brian was furious and he couldn't stop talking about the accident. After a couple of hours, he even accused Frank of trying to kill him. He couldn't understand how Frank could have made a mistake like this and was suddenly convinced that Frank had seen to it deliberately that the beam wasn't properly fixed to the ceiling.

I told him I didn't think that it was deliberate.

'It was an accident,' I said, 'but it shouldn't have happened and the only thing that we can be grateful for is that no one got hurt — or worse.'

We went out into the garden. The swimming pool and the garden were lit up and the evening was warm and inviting.

'Anna, take a deep breath and look around. Have you ever seen anything more lovely than this?'

'No, it's enchanting,' I agreed. 'It's almost like a fairytale garden. I want to stay here for ever and ever ... with you.'

Brian hugged me and we stood quietly and enjoyed the wonderful evening.

'Do you want to go for a walk?' Brian asked.

'Mmmm ...' I answered.

We strolled in the garden with Emily and Luther at our heels, stopping to look at the roses and enjoy their scent.

Brian was holding my hand with a firm grip and I could tell that he was still upset, although trying to hide it. After an hour, we decided to go back into the house and cuddle with the puppies.

Brian stopped outside for a while and lay down on the lawn to play with Luther while Emily and I went into the kitchen to look after the puppies. I lifted up one at a time and stroked them. Brian and I always tried to be fair to them and give all three the same amount of attention. We didn't want to treat any of them differently.

Today, I wonder why we got three puppies at the same time? We hadn't thought it through. We were young and wanted to have as many dogs as possible, without thinking about the consequences. Lots of children and lots of dogs.

Brian dreamed of having a big, noisy family. He wanted the house to be as it was when Christopher Robin lived there. But he didn't want any child of his to be as lonely as Christopher Robin was.

'There's a special magic in the house,' Brian used to say. 'I think our children will inherit it and I'm sure that they'll be as happy here as I am.'

It was late and the puppies were tired and they soon went to sleep. I smiled when I saw the three of them sleeping in a furry bundle. They were adorable. Brian came in and we stood together and looked at them for a while. Luther joined us and lay down in front of their playpen.

Emily sat down in the doorway waiting for us to go to bed. She happily followed us up the stairs and lay down at the foot of the bed with a content sigh while Brian and I brushed our teeth and got ready for bed.

We crawled between the sheets and Brian put on the latest Bob Dylan album, and when the last note was played we were already sound asleep. But not for long.

*   *   *

When I woke up on Monday morning, I knew that Frank was on his way back to Cotchford Farm after spending the weekend with his family.

Brian had had a bad night, tossing and turning next to me. When he eventually woke me up, I found him leaning over me.

'How do you think Frank will react when I tell him what happened?' Brian suddenly said in to the darkness.

'I'm sure he'll come up with some kind of excuse,' I answered and yawned.

'He's well paid and he's got a good job. I'm sure this was no accident. Maybe he hoped the beam would hit *me* in the head.'

'It's nothing to joke about,' I said.

'I'm not. Frank must have known that the beam was going to fall down,' Brian insisted.

'I think you're over-reacting,' I said. 'Please, let's go to sleep.'

Brian didn't drop off again until much later that night, but when I woke up he was sleeping soundly.

I went into the bathroom and got dressed. As soon as I was

ready to go down to the kitchen, Emily suddenly decided to wake up. She stretched out, yawned and jumped off the bed to follow me down the stairs.

Mrs Hallett was already in the kitchen and she'd seen the beam on the floor.

'How could the beam fall from the ceiling? How in the world can anything like this happen?' Mrs Hallett asked me.

'They obviously didn't do a very good job,' I said and explained what had happened the night before.

'Oh, dear me!' Mrs Hallett exclaimed. 'Did anyone get hurt? Is Mr Jones all right?'

'Yes, we were lucky,' I said. 'If it wasn't for Brian I'd probably be dead by now.'

'Oh, dear Lord!' Mrs Hallett said, and put her hands to her cheeks. Then she reached out to hold me. 'My dear, dear child, I'm so pleased you're not hurt. I've always told Mr Jones to be careful and not allow anybody in the house. I've always thought he's far too kind-hearted. And I don't mind saying, Anna, Mr Jones should be more careful with Frank.'

'I know,' I agreed. 'I think he's been too indulgent, but this time it's gone too far.'

Mrs Hallett wanted to make breakfast for Brian, but she knew that was my responsibility, so she restricted herself to asking if there was anything she could do. She behaved as if *she* was to blame for the beam falling down.

'Please, Mrs Hallett, what happened isn't your fault,' I said. 'Sit down and keep me company while I have a cup of tea.'

Mrs Hallett followed me to the dining room; neither of us wanted to sit in the kitchen.

'It's too easy for Mr Jones to be friendly,' Mrs Hallett said. 'He has a soft heart and people take advantage of that. I really hope he can put his foot down this time. I don't like it one little bit.'

Mrs Hallett looked upset and shook her head. She was a

beautiful woman with her heart in the right place. She radiated goodness and honesty and I sometimes wished that I could sit on her knee and be consoled, like a child. She was that kind of person.

We had a nice breakfast together and then I prepared Brian's tray and took it upstairs. Brian was awake, but still in bed. I could tell from his expression that he was in a bad mood.

'Have you seen Frank yet?' he asked.

'No,' I said. 'But I had a long chat with Mrs Hallett and told her what happened. She thinks that you've got to be firmer and not give in this time.'

'What else did she say?'

'She said that you've been too nice.'

'I know,' Brian sighed. 'I suppose it's all my fault.'

'Don't be stupid,' I said. 'It's not your fault that the beam fell down. How could it be?'

'I should have checked everything better.'

'You hired an expert to get things done,' I said. 'You can't be expected to check everything; you haven't got the knowledge or the skill.'

Brian ate his breakfast slowly, lost in his own thoughts.

'I won't except any apologies this time,' he said suddenly, with a determined edge to his voice.

'That's the spirit,' I said smiling. 'Stand up for yourself. This is your house, not theirs. Don't let Frank get away with anything!'

Brian finished his breakfast and jumped out of bed and played some Credence Clearwater Revival, a sound which always seemed to imbue him with lots of energy. He got dressed in his usual beige trousers and a T-shirt, gave me a kiss and went downstairs with an air of conviction.

Soon, I could hear loud voices issuing from the ground floor. I sneaked down the stairs and hid myself in the dining room. I didn't want to get too close to Brian and Frank who were arguing in the kitchen.

'What the hell is all this about?' Brian shouted. 'Did you want to kill me? Or Anna? Or maybe Mrs Hallett? You examined the work and approved it. How the hell could you do that? I ought to report you for attempted murder!'

'I did approve the work,' Frank agreed calmly. 'It looked OK to me.'

'If it was OK, why the hell did the beam fall down? How can you call yourself a builder? You're no better than an apprentice!'

'Look, I'm sorry for what happened,' Frank said, 'but it was an accident. I'll see to it that the beam is properly supported, but it's going to cost a bit.'

'I COULDN'T CARE LESS WHAT IT COSTS. THAT'S YOUR PROBLEM,' Brian screamed, 'AND HERE'S ANOTHER ONE FOR YOU — YOU'RE FIRED! Understood? And you can count on it that I'm going to see that you never work again. EVER!'

Frank remained quite still and silent.

'And for your information,' Brian continued, 'I talked to Fred yesterday and asked him to send me copies of your bills. I'm going to bring in another builder and let him see if they've been fair. I'm not going to let you get away with it this time! And that goes for the bills from the grocery store as well. I thought I'd better look through them, too. Now, get your so-called workmen in here and see to it that they do a proper job this time. If not, I'll sue you, and, I mean it! You almost killed Anna with your carelessness and I'll never forgive you for that! Ever!'

Brian stormed out of the kitchen. He caught sight of me in the dining room and made a sign for me to follow him. We went into the music room and Brian started to play his guitar. I listened to him and felt proud that, for once, he'd spoken his mind. I think he was pleased with himself, too.

I thought that Brian had done the right thing and so did Mrs Hallett. She hadn't been comfortable with the situation on the farm and didn't like the way Frank behaved.

After a while, Brian and I moved into the tape room where we sat down on the floor and listened to some of Brian's recordings.

'Anna, listen, this is really, really nice,' Brian said, and he put on a tape from Morocco for the umpteenth time.

'Listen to the pipes ...'

We stayed in the tape room for hours and listened, among other recordings, to Brian and John Lennon playing together. Neither one of us felt like going back into the kitchen, but eventually we had to. We'd both started to feel hungry, so I said to Brian that I'd make a sandwich.

'Anna, would you mind making me one, too?' he asked with his beautiful, sad eyes. 'I don't want to go back in there until the work's finished.'

'Why? You've done nothing wrong. Why do you always blame yourself? This isn't your fault, and you were right to put your foot down.'

'I know,' Brian said. 'But over the last few months Frank and I have seen a lot of each other. I know he's taking liberties, but who can blame him? He is 44 years old, he has a wife and kids and leads an ordinary, and probably boring, life, and then he meets me and catches a glimpse of what it's like to be a rock star. The attention, the young, beautiful girls and the money. Of course he's jealous of me ... wouldn't you be?'

Brian didn't give me a chance to respond.

'Why do you think Frank landed Joan as his mistress? I mean, to be honest, he isn't the best catch around. Joan is a nice girl and I know that she has a difficult marriage, but one of the reasons she's seeing Frank is because he works for the Rolling Stones. He can offer her a chance to experience something out of the ordinary, right?'

'I don't want to get married and have children if it'll end up like their marriages,' I said.

'I think it's pretty normal,' Brian said. 'Even if it isn't fair to the other half.'

I shrugged and asked Brian if he would like a drink with his sandwich. He nodded and I went into the kitchen.

The workmen were hammering away at the beam and the kitchen looked a mess. Frank wasn't there and since I didn't want to see him I hurried and made a couple of sandwiches with chicken, lettuce, tomatoes and egg. To please Brian, I mixed my own dressing with lemon, French mustard, salt, pepper and oil. I also took out a bottle of wine from the fridge and scurried back to the tape room.

We enjoyed the sandwiches, but Brian was a bit restless and as soon as he'd had enough he went down to the music room and called Alexis Korner. He told him what had happened and I could hear that Alexis thought he'd done the right thing by blaming Frank.

After some much-needed support from Alexis, Brian rang Fred again and asked him to hurry up with the copies of Frank's bills and the bills from the grocery store.

Late in the afternoon, the noise from the kitchen ceased. I figured that the workmen had finished and Brian decided to go and have a look.

He came back after a while and told me that everything seemed to be all right. I asked if he'd talked to Frank, but he said that he hadn't seen him.

Frank stayed away that evening, not daring to show up for either dinner or drinks. Brian was still upset, but later that night he began wondering about Frank and asked me if I thought that Frank was angry with him.

'Anna, why do you think Frank is behaving like this? Have I done anything wrong?'

'No, you just told him what you thought of his bad work,' I said. 'There's nothing wrong in that. Don't go soft, Brian. You have nothing to feel bad about.'

'Go soft? Me? Never!'

I wasn't convinced. I knew that Brian hated falling out with people and that he always wanted to ask for forgiveness if he thought he'd gone too far.

Brian tried to ring David Bailey and Brion in Morocco that evening. Neither was at home. Finally, he got in touch with Keith Richards and gave him a short summary of the incident.

Keith told Brian that he'd been crazy to let Frank into the house in the first place, and that he'd been too soft in becoming friendly with a man like Frank.

'Never let a cat in the house, it will always return if you treat him nice,' Keith said.

At least, that was what Brian told me he'd said.

*　　　*　　　*

On Tuesday morning, I woke up and felt Brian's arm around me. I knew from his breathing that he was awake.

'Did you have another bad night?' I asked.

'Yes. It's really awkward. Frank will probably find out that I've stopped his payments today or, at the latest, tomorrow. I hope he'll understand why, but I'm not sure.'

'Maybe it would be better if you told him yourself,' I suggested. 'That is, if you want to avoid misunderstandings.'

'I've been thinking,' Brian continued. 'The money isn't only for Frank, it's for his workmen as well. I don't want their families to suffer because of me.'

'Why do you always feel guilty for everything?' I asked.

'I haven't a clue. I always feel bad, even though I know that I have done the right thing. At least I think I have. I feel responsible for all of them.'

'That's because you're you,' I said, 'and maybe because you're getting older and more religious!'

'Older maybe, but not religious! And definitely not when it comes to men like Frank.'

'Enough,' I said. 'I'm going down to make you breakfast. Maybe that'll cheer you up.'

I sensed that Brian wanted a simple solution. He would have preferred to forgive and forget and leave it at that. But at the same time, I could tell that he hadn't forgotten and that he was still upset about the whole thing.

His beautiful face was expressionless, and I knew that he was going over all the possibilities, unable to let it go. He was far from the happy, smiling Brian I was used to.

I went into the bathroom and, after a few minutes, Brian joined me.

'I can't stay in bed,' he said. 'Maybe we can have breakfast together in the music room? A nice cup of tea and toast will do.'

We left the bedroom together and walked downstairs with Emily at our heels.

'If we have any wine in the fridge, please bring me some,' he said before he wandered into the music room.

I felt so sorry for him. He looked really unhappy and I decided to try to cheer him up with a simple cheese omelette.

When everything was ready, I put the tea, milk, juice, omelette and a bottle of wine on the tray and carried it down to the music room.

'Why don't we have breakfast in the garden?' I suggested. 'It's a lovely day.'

'Why not?' Brian said. 'Is Frank around?'

'I haven't seen him. Maybe he's hiding in the bushes waiting for breakfast.'

'I don't think so,' Brian said, frowning.

Brian helped me with the tray and we went out into the garden. The sun was shining out of a clear blue sky; it really was a beautiful morning.

'Do you want me to bring out the puppies?' I asked Brian, and his face lit up for a second.

'Yes, please do!' he exclaimed and gave me a kiss.

I went into the kitchen and fetched the puppies. They were so happy and wagged their little tails when I let them out into the garden. They loved to play on the lawn.

'Why don't you put on a pair of shorts and enjoy the sun?' I asked when I got back. 'You're white as a sheet.'

'I know,' he said. 'I just have to look at you to see the difference, but I don't feel like it. When we go to Portugal in August, I promise to lie in the sun and get a tan. Look, I'm sorry if I'm moody, but I'm still really angry ... but it's got nothing to do with you. I'm angry with myself. I've been a fool and trusted people I shouldn't have. When I moved down here I wanted to get to know ordinary people, I thought they were better. I was wrong. The one I know and trust is Mrs Hallett ... and you, of course,' he said, leaning towards me and giving me a kiss.

We ate our breakfast and played with the puppies. Brian's mood soon brightened and eventually he was laughing at the three rascals who were running around on the lawn.

Luther joined them, probably to keep an eye on them, but Emily kept her distance.

After a while, it was time for the puppies to have a nap and we brought them back into the kitchen. The day was getting hotter by the minute and we decided to take a swim.

Brian undressed and dived into the swimming pool. I don't like diving and usually just sit down on the edge and slip in. Brian loved swimming and soon he was back to his old self again. Laughing with joy in the warm water, he could never resist showing off and wanted me to look at him while he did different tricks.

Suddenly, he disappeared from the surface and I looked

around, wondering what he was up to. Minutes passed but there was no sign of him. I started to get worried and decided to get out of the pool to get a better look. I swam towards the edge, but before I reached it, Brian suddenly appeared again. He shook his head and laughed.

'Did I scare you?'

'Yes, you did, and it's not funny,' I fought back tears.

'I'm sorry,' Brian said and took me into his arms. 'I didn't mean to scare you. Forgive me, please?'

Of course I forgave him, he often tricked me like that, but I still remember the horror I felt when I thought that something had happened to him.

We got out of the water and I decided to lie down by the swimming pool to read while Brian went back to the music room. It was quiet and there was no sign of Frank, which was a relief.

An hour or so later, I went back into the house to get dressed. Brian emerged from the music room and followed me upstairs.

'Would you like to go for a ride?' he asked.

'Why, is there something we need to get?'

I walked into the bathroom and rummaged through the wardrobe. I picked up a skirt and then tried to find a matching blouse.

'Here, take this,' Brian said and held out a T-shirt for me. 'It's too small for me, and probably too big for you! But if you like it, you can have it.'

I liked it and I put it on.

'Are you ready?' Brian asked.

'Yes, where are we going?'

Before he could answer, the telephone rang. He chatted for a bit, and when he put the phone down, it rang again. And it continued ringing.

I lay down on the bed and started to read again, and when

Brian had finally finished his calls, it was too late to go anywhere.

Frank did not show up for dinner but Brian had yet another reason to be sour with him. The night before, a friend of Frank and Tom called Janet had arrived to stay with Frank in the apartment above the garage. Brian was furious when he heard that Janet had come down to Cotchford Farm without his permission to stay for a couple of days.

'I'm sick and tired of Frank taking it for granted that he can use this place as he pleases,' Brian shouted. 'Damn it, I'm not running a hotel business where Frank can entertain his girlfriends whenever he likes!'

But later that evening, Brian's conscience troubled him again. He asked me if I really thought he'd done the right thing in stopping Frank's payments. I assured him that he'd had every right to find out what he was paying for, since he suspected that Frank had been cheating him.

'If Frank has nothing to hide, there is no reason for him to be upset,' I added.

We had a quiet dinner, just the two of us. We then played with the puppies and watched TV before going to bed.

Later that night, Brian told me what he'd had in mind when he'd suggested going for a ride that afternoon.

'There's this little church I wanted you to see,' he said. 'I've got a feeling you'll like it. But it doesn't matter ... we'll have plenty of opportunities to go there.'

But we didn't. We had just one day left.

CHAPTER THIRTEEN

On Wednesday morning, 2 July, I went down to the kitchen as usual to prepare Brian's breakfast, and had a chat with Mrs Hallett while I was frying the bacon and eggs. Everything was quite normal.

Brian was smiling when I served him breakfast and seemed a lot calmer than the night before. Frank hadn't been seen anywhere. I was later told that he'd gone up to London.

Brian and I had a nice day. I lay by the swimming pool reading, and Brian was playing in the music room. In the afternoon, we took a walk with the dogs and enjoyed yet another lovely summer's day. It was so peaceful, punctuated only by the birdsong and the sound of the vegetables growing! Brian proudly picked a carrot to show me how much it had grown in a few days.

A little later, Brian began feeling troubled again and started to examine his angry outburst in minute detail all over again. He kept asking me if I thought he should try talking to Frank to clear the air. I simply told him to do what he felt was best for him, but I hoped that he would stand up for his principles. If anyone should have apologised, I reasoned that it should have been Frank, not Brian.

We had a light meal and shared a bottle of wine, and when we'd finished we cleared the table. Then we returned to the dining room to watch *Rowan and Martin's Laugh-In* with Goldie Hawn. Brian loved the American comedienne; he thought that she was beautiful and funny and he never missed a show. He laughed a great deal and sipped at his wine.

When the show had finished, we got ready for bed, but Brian suddenly changed his mind.

'I need to talk to Frank,' he said. He looked worried. 'He must understand why I'm doing this. I need to make him understand. I don't want him to bear any ill will towards me, and it's not fair of him to treat me like an idiot.'

'I think you did the right thing,' I said. 'But I can understand if Frank is hurt and feels insulted.'

'I'm not going to let Frank get away with what he did,' Brian said, 'But I still want him to understand why I fired him and stopped the payments.'

'Why is it so important for you to be friends with Frank? Are you afraid of him, or what?'

'You can never trust a man like Frank. He's a tough guy and I'm sure he's furious with me. But at the same time, he's still dependent on me because I could ruin his career, so I don't think he's stupid enough to take things further.

'I'm going to invite him over for a drink and a swim,' Brian added. 'I want to settle this, once and for all.'

'But it's late,' I said. 'It's almost a quarter past ten.'

'He's awake, I'm sure of that,' Brian said. 'I'll be back shortly.'

Brian disappeared from the dining room and I sighed deeply.

I wanted Brian to have left things as they were until the morning, but he was impulsive and I knew that nothing I could say would have made him change his mind.

A good 15 minutes later, Brian came back with Frank and Janet, whom I'd never met before. We sat down in the dining room for a drink. Frank drank vodka as usual, Brian had a glass of brandy and I stuck to my wine. I don't remember what Janet drank, if anything.

The atmosphere was strained. Frank didn't say anything, he just sat there with his drink, sulking. Brian was light-hearted, trying to cheer Frank up.

'I'm not mad at you any more,' Brian said. 'I just want you to try to understand me. What if the beam had hit Anna? What if she'd died? You understand why I was upset, don't you?'

Frank muttered something which I didn't catch because I was chatting with Janet. I got the impression that she would have preferred to have been left alone in the apartment.

'I've got a lot on my mind,' she said. 'I need to be alone to think things through. I'm not sure what to do about my situation.'

After a while, Brian wanted to swim and we all stood up. I think Frank changed into his swimming trunks in the kitchen, but Brian undressed on the spot. He was already wearing his multi-coloured trunks. I'd taken the opportunity to change into my red bikini bottoms while I was waiting for Brian to get back from Frank's apartment so I just took off my T-shirt. Janet was the only one who didn't feel like swimming.

The garden was as beautiful as ever. The floodlighting around the swimming pool and the garden made the whole place magical. The water was turquoise and shimmered invitingly.

Brian placed his inhaler by the side of the pool, as he always did, and dived in from the springboard while Frank and I slipped in from the edge. Brian was in his element and happily he performed his tricks and laughed. He teased Frank and told him to cheer up. But Frank continued sulking, which made Brian even more mischievous. He couldn't resist pulling Frank's leg.

I saw Brian dive in and the next second Frank's head disappeared underwater. I immediately knew why, Brian loved to grab people's legs and pull them under. Frank soon bobbed to the surface, coughing and spluttering, while Brian had a good laugh.

'Don't be such a sour puss, old man!' Brian teased.

'Nobody calls me an old man!' Frank retorted angrily.

'But you *are* an old man,' Brian said and laughed. 'Old and cranky!'

'And you are nothing but a stuck-up, no-good whimpering rock star!' Frank shouted.

'It's better than being a builder,' Brian called back. 'I have more money, and the birds chase me, not the other way round!'

Frank was furious but Brian carried on teasing him. I told Brian to ease off, but he wouldn't listen.

'He's old enough to take a joke,' Brian said. 'I'm just kidding around and he knows it.'

I wasn't convinced. I knew from earlier instances that Frank took things personally, particularly when Brian was involved, and I didn't like the tense atmosphere that still pervaded.

After a while, Brian swam over to Frank, who saw his chance and pushed Brian's head underwater. Brian had fallen for the same trick he himself had used on Frank.

Brian broke the surface coughing and laughing. He hadn't taken Frank's attack personally.

Brian continued to taunt Frank and I tired of listening to them. I swam to the shallow end of the pool to do some exercise in the water while they stayed in the deep end teasing each other.

I thought about Brian's desire for a reconciliation with Frank and felt that it seemed to be unrealistic, at least for now. My musing was interrupted by Janet.

'Anna, you're wanted on the telephone,' Janet called from the house.

'Coming!' I called back and swam across the pool to the ladder.

Brian caught up with me.

'Hurry back,' he whispered. 'Don't stay away too long. I'll be waiting for you.'

He gave me a kiss as I climbed up the ladder, and walked across the lawn to the dining room door. I didn't know then that it would be the last time I'd see Brian alive.

I met Janet outside and told her I'd take the call in the bedroom.

'Could you please put the receiver down in the kitchen?' I asked, and Janet said she would.

I went up the stairs, lifted the receiver and said hello.

The line was dead.

'Hello!' I said again.

Still no answer. I thought the line had been cut when Janet had hung up in the kitchen, so I took off my bikini bottoms and put on my black briefs. While I was searching for a clean T-shirt, the telephone rang again.

I went back to the bed and answered it. It was my Swedish girlfriend Terry, who was calling from London. I sat down on the bed and leaned against the wall. I assumed that she'd been the previous caller, but I didn't ask her.

Terry told me the latest gossip from London and I told her what had been happening at the farm. We'd been chatting for about ten minutes when I suddenly heard Janet shouting hysterically from below the bedroom window.

'Anna! Anna! Something's happened to Brian!'

I was struck with terror and without saying another word to Terry I dropped the receiver on the bed and rushed off towards the stairs. When I reached the bottom I discovered Frank in the kitchen. He was standing between the kitchen and the dining room with a towel around his shoulders. His head was bent slightly forward and I noticed that his hands were shaking so badly he had trouble lighting a cigarette. He must have heard Janet's cry, but he didn't even look up as I ran past him.

Janet was still standing outside the house as I ran as fast as I could across the lawn to the swimming pool. The surface of the water was as smooth as glass but I couldn't see Brian anywhere. I didn't understand why until I reached the edge.

Brian was lying spread-eagled on the bottom of the pool.

The terror I felt when I saw him will never leave me. The memory still haunts me, day and night. It was nightmarish to see him lying motionless beneath the surface of his beloved pool.

Without thinking, I dived into the water and swam in panic to the bottom. I managed to get a firm grip underneath Brian's arms and began forcing my way to the surface with powerful strokes. I don't know where I got the strength from; I guess I got assistance from above.

When I reached the surface, I held Brian's head above the water and swam towards the edge of the pool. I suddenly felt my strength evaporate and Brian started to slip away from me. I need help, I thought in panic, as I realised we had a matter of minutes to save Brian's life. It never occurred to me that it was already too late.

'Frank, please help me!' I cried out. 'Please help me!'

I saw Frank walking towards the pool. He was in no hurry. He was taking his time and I cried out for his help once more. I was exhausted and scared out of my wits. I didn't want to let Brian slip down to the bottom again.

When Frank reached the edge of the pool he sat down and slipped into the water. Then he helped me pull Brian up on to the edge.

'Why didn't you help Brian? Why did you leave him alone in the pool?' I shouted to Frank. 'It's your fault! I hate you!'

Frank was as cold as ice. He didn't show any sympathy and I noticed that he'd stopped shaking. He didn't respond to my accusations either.

Janet came running towards us when Frank and I turned Brian on to his front to try to get the water out of his lungs. She said that the telephone was out of order.

Frank stood up and started walking towards the house. Janet, whom I later discovered was a trained nurse, helped me to lay Brian flat on his back, and sank down on her knees and started heart massage while I tried to give Brian the kiss of life.

'Why didn't you help Brian?' I sobbed. 'Why didn't you pull him out instead of calling for me? How the hell could you leave him there? What's wrong with you? And where were you when it happened?'

I probably said worse things than that, but I was shocked and terrified and I couldn't understand why Janet had come running to the house instead of jumping into the swimming pool when she saw Brian in trouble. It was completely inexplicable.

Later, I was told that Janet couldn't swim.

'I was strolling around in the garden,' Janet said. 'I saw Brian when I passed the swimming pool and that's when I started calling for help.'

I could not stop myself. I accused both Frank and Janet of leaving Brian without any help when they both knew he was in trouble. I was convinced that between the two of them, at least one knew what had actually happened. And I was convinced that Brian hadn't drowned without someone's intervention.

Janet later said to the police that she'd been in the music room when Brian drowned.

Janet eventually stopped the heart massage, but I fought for Brian's life until the ambulance and the police arrived. I suddenly thought I felt Brian's hand grip mine and I told Janet so.

Janet shook her head and said, 'Anna, it's no use. You've lost him. He's gone. There's nothing you can do.'

I refused to believe her and threw myself over Brian's body. He was wet, but he was still warm and he looked like he was sleeping, a calm, soothing sleep. He couldn't be dead, I said to myself. He'll soon open his eyes and smile happily at me, as he always does.

I was in shock, beside myself with grief, and confused. I felt terribly helpless and lonely. I couldn't stop crying. I felt guilty at having left Brian in the pool. I shouted at Frank and asked him why he had left Brian alone. He didn't answer. And I was too upset to remember exactly what had happened after Janet's cry for help.

It was not until the following day that the truth dawned on me.

*   *   *

I don't remember how long it was that I lay with Brian at the edge of the pool, but I know I was still there when the ambulance driver and the doctor arrived. Someone gripped me firmly and tried to pull me away from Brian, but I refused to be parted from him and clung on while the male nurses put the body on a stretcher and carried it to the ambulance.

I didn't want Brian to leave Cotchford Farm. He belonged there. I wanted him to stay in his beloved home.

'I'm sorry, love.' I heard a male voice say. 'You can't do anything for him. You have to accept that he's dead.'

That was the first time I heard the word 'dead'. It sounded so final. I cried hysterically when the male nurses eventually put the stretcher into the ambulance. The next thing I remember is someone putting a towel round my shoulders. I hadn't realised that I only had my briefs on.

After that, my memories are blurred. I remember one of the policemen saying something to me, but I can't remember if I was questioned or not. I don't think I was. I was too upset and couldn't stop crying. I missed Brian terribly and the only thing I wanted was to be with him.

Later, I was brought up to the bedroom by a couple of strangers who stayed with me. I wanted to be left alone and I managed to make them leave the bedroom for a short while. Even though I was in shock, I was fully aware of the fact that the police might draw the wrong conclusions if they found my Mandrax and Durophet, and I wanted to put my pills in my handbag so I could keep a close eye on them.

While I was alone in the bedroom, Jim Carter-Fea rang to have a chat. Crying, I told him what had happened, that Brian was dead and that I suspected foul play. Later, I found out that Jim, who had called from his club Revolution, had walked back into the premises and turned off the effect lights, before telling his guests the tragic events of the night, that Brian Jones was dead.

The next thing I remember was a local doctor coming up to the bedroom. I was in bed with Emily at my side. He tried to give me an injection of some sedative, but I didn't want him to touch me. I shouted at him.

'Leave me alone! I don't want to die! If you touch me I'll report you!'

I'm not sure why I thought he was going to kill me, but I was scared out of my wits. I was convinced that Brian's death was due to foul play. There is no way that my beloved Brian, who was like a fish in the water, could have drowned, and in my confused state I was scared of being the next victim.

I remember asking the doctor where Brian was and he told me that they had driven him to the local hospital. In my mind, I saw terrifying pictures of the post mortem examination room.

'What are they going to do to Brian?' I sobbed.

'Don't think about that right now,' the doctor answered. 'Try to rest. Tomorrow is another day and you'll need all your strength.'

It was easy for him to say. I was beside myself with grief and I burst into tears. I don't think I've ever felt as lonely as I did that night. I didn't have any close relatives to comfort me. I didn't even have any friends nearby. I felt alone and abandoned, except for the doctor who stayed with me all night.

I couldn't sleep, and during the night I heard people on the ground floor. It sounded as if they were having a party. There were loud voices and a lot of activity. I don't know who they were or what they were doing in the house. It almost felt as if the house had been invaded by aliens.

The next day, I was told that Tom Keylock had arrived at Cotchford Farm some time during the night. I couldn't work out why he was there. Brian had left the Stones, they had nothing to do with him any more. Why didn't Brian's parents come to the house? Brian was their son, he wasn't the property of Rolling Stones Inc.

I suspect that Frank had rang Tom and told him that Brian was dead, but I'm not sure he told Tom the whole truth.

Sometime during the night, I heard someone open the bedroom door.

'Is Anna asleep?' an unfamiliar voice asked.

'Yes,' the doctor said and squeezed my hand.

'No,' I whispered almost to myself. I didn't have the strength to speak up.

I blamed myself for the tragedy all night and I remember the doctor telling me not to. He said that none of it had been my fault. I didn't agree. If I hadn't left Brian alone in the pool with Frank, he would still be alive. It *was* my fault that he was dead.

THE END

'You're young and strong,' the doctor said. 'Life goes on and time heals all wounds.'

He patiently listened when I told him about Brian, about things we'd done and planned to do, and about what we were going to do in the future. I knew Brian was dead, but I refused to accept it. I told myself that I was only having a bad dream and that I'd soon wake up with Brian by my side.

At the same time, I felt a chill suffuse my body. It was an iciness that would protect me. It was a remarkable, ice-cold calmness. It wasn't me any more. My other self took over.

Many years on, I would repress the memories of my life with Brian. Deny them. Then, if someone asked me about Brian, it wouldn't hurt me. I protected myself by denying that I'd been the Rolling Stone, Brian Jones', girlfriend. I'd been Brian's girlfriend. Nothing more.

When all the newspapers carried the stories of Brian's death and my name was mentioned in connection with his, it wasn't as if they were talking about Brian and me — it was about two completely different people.

Everything was unreal. I said virtually nothing and felt frightened. And I continued to blame myself for Brian's death. The words *'If I hadn't left him in the pool with Frank, he'd still be alive,'* still haunt me.

I've lived with my sense of guilt for 30 years. I know I'm not to blame for what happened to Brian, but that's no consolation.

I also feel guilty for not telling the truth earlier, for not defending Brian, for allowing all these lies to be circulated without objecting.

There are times when I feel that Brian is the one who got away lightly.

CHAPTER FOURTEEN

THE
COVER-UP

The morning after Brian's death, I stayed in bed trying to piece together exactly what had happened the evening before, and when I did, I suddenly felt sick.

Frank's odd behaviour surrounding the incident aroused my suspicions. He'd been close to the pool and should have been there before me. But instead of reacting immediately to Janet's screams, he'd remained between the kitchen and the dining room and, with shaking hands, had tried to light a cigarette. Why hadn't he run to the pool when he heard Janet's cry for help? There is only one answer to that question: Frank must have known it was too late.

It is also difficult to explain his reluctance to help me get Brian out of the pool, his strangely cold behaviour and the lack of sympathy or concern when I tried to save Brian's life.

There was no doubt in my mind. Frank had killed Brian. He'd finally lost his self-control.

Brian had made a fatal mistake when he insisted on teasing Frank, despite my pleas for him to stop. His wish had finally come true. He'd made Frank mad enough to snap. But at what price? Brian had paid for it with his life.

My suspicions were confirmed later that day.

Tom Keylock and Frank had one mutual problem — Janet. They had to explain who she was and what she was doing at the farm. They were both married with families.

At the inquest, Frank told the police that Janet had been an occasional girlfriend for a couple of months, and she confirmed it.

I assume Tom first learned the truth about Brian's death when he sat at Frank's deathbed and made him sign a confession. I hope, for Tom's sake, that he didn't withhold the truth to save Frank from imprisonment.

From the minute Tom arrived at Cotchford Farm, he took control of the house. When I woke up in the morning, he wandered into the bedroom and closed the curtains. Under no circumstances was I allowed to look out of the window.

When he left the room, I couldn't resist looking outside. The driveway was crowded with people. Hundreds of journalists and photographers were waiting for something to happen.

I ran back to bed and Emily pressed herself against me. I was glad she was with me. She was the only consolation I had. I don't know what I would have done without her.

I called my girlfriends, Terry and Linda, and asked them to come down to the farm. They showed up a couple of hours later and it felt good to have friends close by.

Tom came up to the bedroom towards mid-day. He informed me that the police wanted to interview me, Frank and Janet. I told him I wasn't well enough to talk to anybody, but Tom insisted.

To avoid the photographers, I dressed as a boy and we were

walked secretly through the garden to a waiting car, while Terry and Linda walked out through the front door. The photographers and journalists had never seen me with Brian, and they mistook Linda, who was blonde, for me.

I was scared and alone in a foreign country and I couldn't prove that Frank had killed Brian. I still blamed myself for Brian's death. I shouldn't have left him in the pool. Why did I? Why hadn't I stayed with him? Why? Why? Why? I wanted to cry out my grief and my loss. But nothing I did would bring Brian back to me.

We were driven down to the police station in East Grinstead, and as we got out of the car, Frank sidled up to me.

'Don't forget to tell them it was Brian who wanted me to come down to you, not me.'

'He felt guilty and wanted to make it up to you,' I said.

I didn't understand Frank's comment. I still don't. It didn't matter whether Brian had asked him over or not, did it?

'Just think about what you say to the police,' Frank said.

'The only thing you need to tell them is that Brian had been drinking and that his drowning was an accident. You don't have to tell them anything else. I left Brian to go to the kitchen and light a cigarette and I don't know any more than you,' Frank added. 'But there's no need for you to tell the police that you saw me in the kitchen. Just tell them we pulled Brian out of the pool together.'

I could see that Frank was worried, and I knew he had every reason to be. But I was scared, too. I didn't want to end up like Brian, so I did what Frank had told me to do.

I didn't dare challenge Fate.

*   *   *

Frank lied during the interview.

Janet's recollections seemed confused.

And I concealed the truth.

Today, I'm ashamed for not telling the whole truth, but I was scared and still in shock. I knew that everybody would blame Brian and his earlier problems with drugs and alcohol. Nobody would step forward and tell the police that Brian was clean from drugs and that he didn't have a drink problem.

I now know that the autopsy showed that Brian had taken some kind of drug, but it was a surprise to me. The only pills he had were Valium, Mandrax and ten Durophet, and I know that he was scared of taking any of them. He was terrified of becoming dependent again. I wondered if he'd taken Durophet without me knowing it. Or had someone slipped a pill into his drink? I don't know. But I still wonder what kind of drug the coroner found in his body.

Maybe I shouldn't have interpreted Frank's suggestion as a threat. But I did.

*   *   *

In the aftermath of Brian's death, there was a lot of speculation about a conspiracy. The Stones had nothing to gain from Brian's death, had they? The only one who would have gained was Frank, particularly, if his invoices were shown to be dodgy.

I still don't understand why Frank didn't admit to killing Brian. How could he live with himself, knowing what he had done? What about his conscience, or feelings for me and Brian's parents? I'll never understand Frank, or his motives.

When I look back today, I also feel that it was wrong to make me attend an interview at the police station the day after Brian's death. I was in shock. I'd lost my boyfriend, the man I loved. I just wanted to know where he was. Was he really dead? Or was everything just a bad dream? I was in a state of total confusion.

I remember that Frank, Janet and I were shown into different rooms at the police station. I also remember crying during the interview and I recall the room being cold and impersonal. My only comfort was Emily, who faithfully sat by my side. I refused to be parted from her.

I didn't lie to the police who questioned me, but I didn't tell them the whole truth. I know I let Brian down. I'm still ashamed of withholding information, but I was afraid of reprisals. And as things went on, I felt I was spiralling down into a dark and lonely pit of depression.

I knew Brian's drowning was not an accident. But what could I do?

*   *   *

After the initial interview, I was taken back secretly to the house. I went straight up to the bedroom. The house was full of strangers and I didn't have the strength to talk to them. I didn't know what they were doing there and I didn't care.

I lay down on the bed with Emily by my side, staring at the ceiling. Emily knew something was wrong and she licked my hand and pressed her little body close to mine. I patted her and vowed I'd look after her.

Tom said that I could have Emily. I found out later that they'd given Emily, Luther and the puppies away to somebody. At least, that's what I've been told. I'll never forgive Tom, I'd lost Brian, and he could have let me keep Emily at the very least. She was the only one I had left.

I'd been lying on the bed for at least an hour when Tom came into the bedroom.

'A car is coming down from London to pick you up,' he said.

I remember I was really upset by Tom's behaviour which to me seemed to show insufficient sympathy. He'd been making decisions about everything. I wished Brian's parents were there instead of the lot who were going through the house. If I'd been stronger, I would have told them all to go to hell.

Few showed me any consideration, extended their condolences, asked me how I was or expressed their sympathy.

Tom stayed in the room with me and told me to pack a bag with the things I needed. He said that I wasn't allowed to take too much.

'The police are coming by later today to examine the house,' he said. 'Everything has to be as it was yesterday. You'll have to come back and get your stuff.'

I didn't know how the legal system worked in England and so I didn't object.

I tried to pack a suitcase. He said I could only take a few things. I didn't know what to pack.

Eventually, I succeeded in smuggling a few of Brian's favourite shirts, a coat and one of his hats into my bag. I couldn't add anything else because the bag was full. I had to leave as I was, but I thought I'd be back at Cotchford Farm in a couple of days. I didn't think that I'd never see my personal belongings or my clothes again. If I'd known that, I would have refused to leave the house altogether.

Brian's shirts were a comfort to me for a long time. I pressed them to my face when I was going to sleep to breathe in Brian's scent. They were my only consolation. Years went by before I washed them, and I did so reluctantly.

Sitting in the car before leaving Cotchford Farm, I didn't know what to expect, or even where I was being taken.

I was driven straight to the Stones' office where I waited. At least an hour passed before anyone talked to me.

I saw Bill Wyman, Charlie Watts and the new guitarist, Mick Taylor, and wondered where Mick Jagger and Keith Richards were. Later, someone told me that Mick had been taken to hospital for treatment having heard the news of Brian's death.

It's possible that Keith was in the office, but I didn't see him.

I guess they were as shocked as me, but they also had another problem — the concert at Hyde Park, which was scheduled to take place in a couple of days. Should they cancel it? It was a difficult decision.

Eventually, I was shown into Les Perrin's office. I'd never met the head of the PR department before.

Les introduced himself, as did Bill Wyman and Charlie Watts. None of them offered their condolences, but kept on talking about their new single 'Honky Tonk Women', the concert in Hyde Park and other business affairs; everything, in fact, except Brian.

I was sitting on a sofa watching them. I remember thinking I was glad Brian wasn't there to see his friends behaving like arseholes.

Time passed, and about half an hour later Les came and sat down next to me. At long last, he said how sorry he was, but I doubted his earnestness. The only thing I wanted was to get out of the room and be left alone with my grief.

'Anna,' Bill Wyman said suddenly, 'I think it would be good for you to go to Astrid. She is staying at our hotel. Go there and talk to her. You're both from Sweden and I'm sure she'll be pleased to see you.'

Someone from the office gave me a ride to the Londonderry Hotel where the Stones were staying before their Hyde Park concert.

I remember wearing a pair of white trousers, a black jacket with white stars and a white hat. My eyes were red from crying and I hid them behind a pair of sunglasses.

Astrid's first words to me when I arrived surprised me.

'What a lovely jacket! Where did you buy it?'

I didn't know what to say. It wasn't the welcome I'd expected, considering the circumstances. Maybe she was nervous and unsure of how to behave towards me.

I was weak at the knees when I arrived at the hotel. I'd had a hard time accepting that Brian was no longer with me — it seemed he was suddenly everybody's property. It was eating my heart out. It hurt so much and nobody understood me. I was alone with my grief.

Astrid and I sat down in the bathroom. I don't know why. We chatted for almost two hours before either of us realised that we were speaking in English instead of Swedish. When it dawned on us, we laughed. It felt good.

I got to know Astrid a bit and I liked her. Brian had told me about her and I knew that he'd thought of her; she was a nice girl, who preferred to live a normal life. She wasn't interested in partying or appearing in public.

Later in the evening, I was transferred to a room, or suite, of my own. It was comforting to have Astrid close by, even though I didn't really know her or Bill very well. But Astrid did her best to cheer me up and we spent a lot of time chatting. She was good company and I could overcome my grief for an hour or two.

Astrid's sister and her boyfriend were visiting London and Astrid suggested that we should go shopping with them. She told me to dress as casually as possible to avoid attention. I didn't dress like them. Astrid and the other girls around the Stones wore hippie clothes with long skirts in multi-coloured patterns.

I put on one of Brian's shirts and my white trousers and off we went. We headed for Biba, the only store in London at that time where you could find the latest fashions. I only had about £12, but Astrid gave me some money. I bought two short dresses, one cream-coloured with buttons down the front and on the long sleeves. The other was white with long sleeves. I also bought a white, crocheted suit, which I wore when I went back to East Grinstead to attend the inquest with the coroner. I didn't think about it then, but the suit was almost see-through and the journalists didn't hesitate to criticise me for it.

I spent some time in the company of Astrid and her sister. We had dinner together and they tried to do their best to raise my spirits. Bill was busy with the concert arrangements and was only occasionally at the hotel.

Astrid and Bill were aware of the damage to my mental health and tried to persuade me to see a doctor. I refused. Today, I know I should have followed their advice. I was in need of professional help. My sense of guilt almost suffocated me.

'I don't need a doctor,' I said. 'I'll manage.'

I'd withdrawn into my own inner world. Besides, I didn't trust anyone. My only real friends were my pills, which I had smuggled out from Cotchford Farm. With their help, I avoided a collapse. The whole world seemed unstable. I tried to find some kind of balance and struggled to get through each day, but I felt as if I was walking on balloons. I stumbled and fell now and then, but who cared? My life was over. I didn't have the strength even to think about the future.

Tom Keylock came to check on me occasionally, and each time I asked if he could fetch Emily for me.

It wasn't until after the inquest that I learned that the dogs had been placed in new homes on the day I was brought back to London.

'The dogs are fine,' Tom said when I confronted him. 'You don't have to worry about them.'

I burst into tears. First Brian had been taken from me, and now I'd not see the dogs again. My grief knew no bounds. I couldn't stop thinking about my poor little Emily and Luther, the big baby who'd made us laugh so many times. They were alone without understanding what had happened. They were abandoned by both Brian and me. And what about the puppies? What had happened to them?

I asked Tom when I could go back to the farm to collect my personal belongings and my clothes.

'There's no hurry,' he said. 'The police haven't completed their investigation of the house yet. We'll take care of that when things cool down.'

*   *   *

I spent long hours alone in my suite. It felt like a golden cage. I was told that the press were all over the hotel, day and night, and for my own protection I wasn't even allowed to leave my room unaccompanied.

By Friday evening, I couldn't stand it any longer. I invited Terry and Linda over and we decided to have a quiet dinner together to cheer us up.

I called room service and ordered smoked salmon, shrimps, and three fillets of beef and chips. We were getting ready to sit down when the telephone rang. It was my friend Victor Lownes. I'd called him shortly after Brian's death and he knew I was convinced that Brian had been killed.

'Call a cab and come and see me!' he said excitedly. 'They'll pay you £50,000 for one interview. This is your chance to tell everyone what really happened to Brian!'

'I'll call you back,' I said.

'No!' he insisted. 'Get over here. Don't talk to anybody. Hurry!'

I repeated that I'd be in touch with him later and decided to ring Astrid and ask her advice. I wasn't tempted by the money; it was the opportunity of telling the truth. But I was too scared to do it without support. Astrid said that I had to make the decision myself. She put Bill on the phone and I explained what had happened.

I don't recall exactly what he said, but he asked me to think the matter over before I talked to the press.

'It's easy to say the wrong things,' he concluded.

No more than three minutes after my chat with Bill, a very annoyed Stones aide threw the door open and shouted, 'Follow me!' That's as far as any pleasantries went. His blazing eyes scared me. I couldn't understand why he was behaving like that, and I had no idea where he was taking us.

We took the lift down to the garage and the guy pushed me into a car. Without a word, he drove us to an unfamiliar house in London where he opened the front door and ushered us roughly into a living room.

A dark-haired man stood in the middle of the room and looked at us as we entered. He didn't say a word.

No niceties were exchanged. He didn't even take my hand. Instead, he came straight to the point.

'How much do you want? Is £50,000 enough? Or maybe £100,000? Tell me what you want to keep silent.'

He glared at me.

'What do you take me for?' I shouted back. 'Do you really think that money is the answer?'

I was insulted and hurt.

The guy looked startled. He tried to hide his surprise, but I noted his uncertainty when I declined his offer. He'd thought I was for sale. He was probably used to being able to buy what he wanted. Even silence.

The two men left the room together. I sat down on a sofa and looked around. The room had a thick carpet and soft lighting. It reminded me of a pleasant, impersonal nightclub.

I suddenly felt anxious and didn't know what to do.

A few minutes passed before they returned. I wasn't given any explanations. The Stones aide just said that he was going to drive us back to the hotel.

I don't know what they discussed. I never asked. I was too preoccupied with my own problems. It wasn't until later that I began to wonder why they had had to speak in private.

The guy was silent on the way back. He followed me to the suite and waited for me to go in. When I turned round to close the door, I stared at him.

'You know as well as I do that Brian's death was no accident,' I said and closed the door right in his astonished face.

It felt good.

The food was still on the table where we'd left it. Cold. But it didn't matter. I'd lost my appetite.

I had trouble sleeping that night. I dropped off for an hour and woke up in a cold sweat. The next morning, I felt sick and dragged myself to the toilet where I vomited. I thought it was due to the fact that I hadn't eaten anything the day before, and the after effects of my meeting with the two guys.

*   *   *

On the third day following Brian's death, the Rolling Stones played in Hyde Park. Brian and I had made plans to go to London to see the concert. He'd wanted to show the fans that he and the Stones were still friends, even though he'd left the band. We'd been looking forward to a weekend in London, enjoying a nice meal at one of our favourite restaurants and a visit to one of the clubs.

Many people objected to the concert being staged only three days after the tragedy. I know the Stones discussed the problem again and again, and it was Charlie Watts who came up with the idea of commemorating it to Brian. Bill and Charlie were sincere in their grief and I believe that if it had been up to the two of them the concert would have been cancelled. I still don't know what Mick and Keith felt about Brian's death.

Bill and Astrid invited me to come with them to Hyde Park. I don't know who stopped me, but perhaps someone was afraid that I might run into a journalist.

The situation was precarious, to say the least. If I'd stepped forward and told the press that Brian's death hadn't been an accident, it would have created headlines all over the world, which might have had repercussions for the Stones and which would definitely have thrown a whole new light on Frank Thorogood.

I was a threat.

Instead of going to the concert, I stayed alone in my suite, crying myself to sleep. I felt lonely and abandoned and had no one to talk to, not even my new-found friend Astrid. I was grief-stricken.

Looking back, I realise now that, considering my state of mind, it was probably for the best that I didn't attend the concert. My grief struck too deep and if I'd seen the Stones on the stage it would have emphasised my loss, and that Brian had gone forever.

I don't know if I would have been able to cope with the realisation at that point. I still nourished a faint hope that everything had been a bad dream and that Brian would soon return to me.

*   *   *

Late on Sunday afternoon, the telephone rang. It was Les Perrin who said that he wanted to see me. Terry, who was with me at the time, called for a taxi and we went together to the Stones' office where Les Perrin was expecting me.

He asked me to sit down on the sofa and he sat next to me. Then he confirmed my suspicions. Allan Klein, the Stones' manager, had told him to have a word with me.

'Do you really want to tell a journalist about your life with

Brian?' he asked, and without waiting for my answer, he said, 'Is the money that important to you? Do you think it's right to earn money from Brian's death?'

His words cut deep into me and my eyes filled with tears. I didn't answer. I couldn't. What did he think of me? That I didn't have any feelings for Brian? That I was just with him for the fame and money? How could he be so wrong? How dared he!

'If you want to tell everyone about your life with Brian, I can hand-pick a journalist for you,' Les Perrin added.

The words stuck in my throat. 'Maybe,' I said after a while. 'I have to think about it.'

I had no intention of talking to anyone about Brian or our life together. It was private, and no one else's concern. Not then. Brian was mine. I didn't want to share him with anyone. I wanted to keep my memories to myself.

The only thing I wanted to talk about was his death. To defend him and clear his name. But I didn't dare tell Les Perrin about my intentions.

'I want you to sign this,' Les Perrin suddenly said and held a piece of paper out for me.

I glanced down it. It stated that I was allowed to give an interview on the condition that what I said would not harm Brian or the Rolling Stones. It also stated that Les Perrin was to give copy-approval before it was printed in the paper.

My first reaction was that Les Perrin had been thoughtful, but then I suddenly twigged; what would happen if I gave an interview without telling him? Would he sue me? Or worse? I suddenly felt threatened again.

He didn't want me to sign the agreement to protect me, he was interested in one thing and one thing only. To keep the Stones out of ... what?

What could I possibly say that would harm Brian or the Stones? What did I know that was so dangerous?

It suddenly dawned on me that Les Perrin had no interest whatsoever in finding out what had happened to Brian. His only motive was money and preventing me from saying something that would jeopardise the Stones' future, and, indirectly, his income. He wanted to silence me. But I still didn't understand why I was such a threat.

I signed the agreement. I didn't dare say no.

When Les Perrin had the signed document in his hand, he looked very pleased with himself.

'I'll try to find an apartment for you,' he said. 'I gather that you understand you can no longer stay at Cotchford Farm.'

I nodded.

'You don't have to worry about anything,' Les Perrin added. 'I'll take care of everything.'

He told me that the date for Brian's funeral had been settled. It was to take place on 10 July in his home town of Cheltenham. Les Perrin promised to see to it that someone gave me a lift there.

In spite of Les Perrin's promises about finding me a flat and transport to Brian's funeral, I was incredibly disappointed in him when I left the office. I thought he'd behaved in a very businesslike and offhand manner.

Brian had often talked about Les Perrin and his wife Janie, whom he couldn't resist gossiping about.

'She's extremely curious,' he said. 'She wants to know everything, but I usually just tell her bits and pieces. Sometimes I get the feeling that Les asks her to call me to check on me.'

When I first moved in with Brian he often received phone calls from her.

'Janie is harassing me about you,' he smiled mischievously. 'She's annoyed because I won't tell her about you. She wants to know what you look like, where you were born, everything. I can see her now ... she's ready to burst out of sheer curiosity!'

Janie rang now and then to try to get Brian to reveal more about me. I couldn't avoid hearing snippets of their conversations and sometimes Brian beckoned me to come and listen to her.

'I don't think Les wants me to be happy,' Brian once said. 'He wants me to have problems so he can help me. I think it's a need in him.'

I thought about Brian's words when I left the office. Les Perrin had shown that he was no friend of ours. He had not contacted me to comfort or help me, and if he'd really been a friend, he would have. I think Brian was right all along.

'He is a PR person to his fingertips,' he said. 'Nothing can come between him and his work, neither feelings nor conscience.'

Brian was no fool. He saw through the people he was associated with.

But that didn't mean he didn't like them. He saw something good in everyone and I knew he liked Les Perrin and considered him to be his friend.

My thoughts revolved around Brian and the people he'd been associated with. I realised that he hadn't had many genuine friends, most of them were hangers-on. And I didn't find many instances of true friendship among the people I met after Brian's death.

I'm glad he never found out the truth about his so-called friends.

I was deeply disappointed and at the same time upset when I thought about the Rolling Stones and the people who worked for them, with the exception of Bill and Charlie. I'm certain that Bill was sincerely sorry about what had happened to Brian and I'm grateful to him and Astrid for being there for me over the first difficult days following the tragedy.

The other people I met didn't give me any support, no one

expressed their sympathy or made any effort to help me. I had to take care of myself in the only way I could. Their primary concern seemed to be that I didn't do anything which could jeopardise the Stones' career.

*   *   *

On 7 July, Frank, Janet and I were asked to appear at the coroner's inquest in East Grinstead for the formal hearing.

When I woke up that morning I felt sick again. I had to run to the bathroom where I knelt beside the toilet and threw up. Eventually my stomach settled down, but my legs shook and I wondered whether I'd have the strength to get through the inquest. I was afraid of going to pieces and I took one Durophet hoping it would make me feel better.

I always had my breakfast in my suite and when it arrived and the waiter had started to lay the table with eggs, bacon, juice, toast, cheese and tea, I burst into tears. In my mind, I saw Brian and remembered his sunny smile when I placed the breakfast tray on the bed next to him. I pushed the plate away and left the table.

After a while, the drug should have begun to soothe me, but instead I started getting palpitations. I panicked and swallowed half a Valium and went back to bed.

Terry came to visit me and told me that hundreds of photographers and journalists had gathered outside the hotel. She helped me to get dressed. I chose to wear the white crocheted dress from Biba.

I was picked up by one of the Stones' employees. His name was David Sandison. He was dark and about 30. He said that it was his duty to protect me from the press and see to it that I got to East Grinstead in time for the inquest.

We took the lift down to reception and he put his arm around my shoulder when we stepped out to make us look more like a couple. Since neither the photographers nor the journalists knew what I looked like, they didn't realise who I was until we'd got into the car.

We thought we'd fooled them, but suddenly the car was surrounded by the press. I was terrified and instinctively bent over and covered my face. David started the car and drove away.

When we arrived at East Grinstead, it was chaos. Hundreds of photographers and journalists had gathered outside the building. I couldn't understand why they didn't respect the fact that I was in mourning and when they started screaming and taunting me because of my see-through dress I almost burst into tears.

I still shudder when I think about the circling vultures.

CHAPTER FIFTEEN

B R I A N

I left the car with a killer by my side. Frank had come forward to help me get past the press. He lent me his coat to protect me from the taunting crowd and then he put his arm around my shoulder. I wondered how he had the guts even to touch me, but I was in no position to protest.

The photographers and journalists reminded me of a swarm of locusts. I tried to avoid the cameras by bending my head and I refused to answer the questions shouted at me by the journalists. I wished they'd left me alone. I felt utterly distraught.

Frank seemed unaffected by the commotion. He didn't show any feelings whatsoever. He gave nothing away. During the short walk up to the building, Frank bent down towards me.

'Just tell the coroner the same thing you told the police and everything will be all right.'

I nodded, but I wished I'd had the nerve to blame him publicly for what he had done. Why, Frank? I wondered as we walked. Don't you understand what you've done? Don't you see that you've ruined my life? Can't you see the effect of your actions?

The questions floated around in my mind and I wished I'd had the guts to ask them. I wished I'd had the strength to put my foot down.

Frank's voice hadn't been threatening, but I still felt scared and abandoned, and I didn't dare disobey him.

In retrospect, there are some things about that day I deeply regret. I still feel guilty about letting Brian down and I despise myself for not telling the truth there and then. But the grief. The cruel grief. A consuming, black grief.

*   *   *

When we entered the building, I met Brian's father for the first time. Lewis Jones wore a dark suit, a white shirt and a tie. He was a short man with grey hair and glasses. His features didn't remind me of Brian, who was probably more like his mother, Louise. She wasn't present at the hearing, and I can only assume that she didn't have the strength.

Lewis and I got on well right from the start. We understood each other's grief and loss and I think we would have been friends if Brian had been spared. Lewis then introduced me to Barbara, Brian's younger sister.

I went to the cloakroom and Barbara accompanied me. I felt so sorry for her. She'd been the youngest of three siblings and now she was the only one left.

Barbara embraced me and held my hand. I didn't know what to say. The tears rolled down my cheeks and I excused myself and went into the toilet. I swallowed a Durophet and a Valium. I wouldn't have got through the inquest without my drugs.

It was hot and crowded in the courtroom. I thought about

Frank's request and at the time I didn't care what I said. Brian was dead. Whatever I said, he would never come back to me.

Lewis and Barbara took care of me. I sat between them and they held my hands. I couldn't stop crying and I was grateful to them for being there. They were the first people who understood what I was going through, the first who cared. I wished we'd had the opportunity to meet before Brian had died. I would have liked to talk to them and got to know them better.

Barbara squeezed my hand to encourage me when it was my turn to step forward and answer the coroner's questions.

'This is not true,' I whispered to her when I rose, but I don't know if she understood what I meant. I have a strong feeling that she misinterpreted my comment, thinking I meant that it wasn't true that Brian was dead.

I glanced at Frank when I sat down. He sat erect and stared at me, expressionless. I suppose he was nervous.

My memory of the hearing is hazy. I suppose I told the same story I'd told the police. I later heard the coroner talk about Brian, but I didn't want to listen and convinced myself that he was talking about a stranger, someone I didn't know. I also refused to listen to the autopsy report, shutting the words out. I couldn't take it.

When the inquest was over, and the coroner had said that Brian's death was due to misadventure, I wanted to shout. But I didn't.

I left the courtroom with Lewis and Barbara, and we said goodbye. The last thing Lewis said to me was, 'I'll be seeing you at the funeral.'

It wasn't to be.

*   *   *

After the harrowing experience of the inquest, David drove me back to London and escorted me to my suite. I was alone again with my grief and anxiety. I paced the room restlessly with one of Brian's shirts pressed to my chest. I was convinced that I was losing my mind.

I could neither eat nor relax. Everything felt unreal and strange. I was beside myself with grief and the tears never stopped.

Later that evening, Tom Keylock appeared again.

'I'm going to take you to another hotel where you'll be safe.'

I did what he asked. I didn't seem to have any free will any more. I was like a puppet. It took me just a few minutes to pack my belongings.

Tom took me to a hotel somewhere in the Kensington area. I don't know the name of it, but it was luxurious and I had no reason to complain, except that it was yet another golden cage all over again. I wasn't allowed to leave my room.

'It's for your own good,' Tom said. 'You're not safe out there.'

Not safe? Why? Who was after me? I wanted to ask, but I knew it would have been useless.

My only company was Terry who dropped by in the daytime. It was comforting to have her close by. I knew it must have been boring for her spending time with me, but I was grateful that she did.

I was a mere shadow of my former self. I just cried and felt terrible. Terry hardly recognised me.

The evenings were endless and to make time pass I pretended that I was going out. I took a shower, put on some make-up and dressed up. When I was ready, I called room service and ordered my dinner, which I never even tasted.

The only contact I had with the outside world was through the newspapers which Terry brought me. But the headlines reminded me of what had happened and they only made me cry. On all the front pages I could read about Brian's death and the inquest. I forced myself to read them and realised that no one knew the truth. There were different versions, but none of them were true. The journalists had only one thing in common — they all thought that Brian was depressed and influenced by drugs when he died.

I wanted to defend Brian. I wanted to tell everyone that he'd been happy and at one with the world when he died. I wanted them to know that he'd stopped taking drugs, that he was enjoying his new life. The picture they painted of Brian was unfamiliar, incorrect and, above all, unfair.

I thought about Brian all the time and, at long last, I understood how alone and abandoned he must have felt when he was hidden away while he waited to go to court after the last drug bust the police carried out. He knew he was innocent, but no one around him believed him. He felt he was being used, and that no one had thought of his feelings.

We were both victims. The Rolling Stones had to be protected. No matter what.

*   *   *

On Wednesday afternoon, I was picked up once more without any advance notice and driven to Heathrow Airport to catch a flight to Stockholm.

I objected strongly. I didn't want to go to Sweden. I was going to Brian's funeral. How could they do this to me?

Soon enough I realised that it was no good resisting. My head was spinning. What was I going to do? I had to pay my respects to Brian. I couldn't leave without letting him know I loved him and was aching for him.

Before leaving the hotel, I rang Les Perrin. I told him I wished to offer Brian a token of remembrance at his funeral, and asked him to buy a red rose and a gold charm depicting faith, hope and love, and place them on Brian's coffin. He vowed that he would do it.

His promise was empty.

Later, when I eventually returned to London, I asked Les Perrin about the rose and the charm. I didn't want him to have to pay for my last gift of affection to Brian.

'I couldn't find any jewellery,' he said. 'You don't owe me anything.'

He broke my heart and I'll never forgive him. He deprived me of saying goodbye to the man I loved and he even deprived me of giving my beloved a token of remembrance.

My heart was aching with sorrow when the car took me to the airport. I fervently wished that I could have said my last goodbye to Brian and I didn't understand why Les Perrin wanted to get rid of me so fast. He knew that my residence permit was running out. It was a question of days. Why did he deprive me of my last chance to say goodbye? It was unfeeling and cruel. He just didn't care about me at all. It was clear to me that I had to be whisked away before I said anything that might harm the Stones. I still don't know what that might be. Maybe he knew more about Brian's death than I did.

The document Les Perrin had made me sign scared me, and I didn't dare accept any interviews from the journalists who had been chasing me ever since the tragedy. I was terrified that something would happen to me if I told them what I knew.

I knew that Brian was killed and, deep down, I also knew that the truth would one day be revealed. With or without my help. I just had to be patient. But patience is something young people lack. And I was young.

*   *   *

At the airport, I had the ticket in my hand and someone helped me board the plane. After a while, I was climbing high above London and there I sent a silent prayer to Brian and asked his forgiveness for not attending his funeral. And I gave him a promise to return — as soon as I'd gathered my strength.

*   *   *

On 10 July 1969, my beloved Brian was buried in his home town of Cheltenham. Thousands of mourners followed him to his final rest, while I sat alone in my old nursery in Stockholm crying my heart out.

I had to read about the funeral in a Swedish newspaper the following day; I read a report about the bronze coffin covered with yellow roses in the shape of guitar, Brian's parents and sister, Bill and Charlie from the Rolling Stones and all the fans who had cried for Brian.

I was the only one who was denied my right to say goodbye to my boyfriend. The grief tore me to pieces. My only wish had been to follow Brian to his final rest. But I was denied the right to determine my own actions. That was done for me by Rolling Stones Inc.

The day Brian was buried, a part of me died.

*   *   *

Over the following weeks, I lived like a zombie. I could neither eat nor sleep. The sorrow in my heart went so deep that nobody could comfort me. I sat in my rocking chair, staring at the ceiling.

I lost weight faster than I could ever have thought possible. But I didn't know and I didn't care. It was my mother who forced me to stand on the scales and it showed 6 stones.

'How do you think Brian would feel if he saw you now?' my

mother asked. 'I think he'd be really worried about you. You have to pull yourself together. You're hurting yourself and others.'

I tried to eat, but it wasn't easy. The mere thought of food made me feel sick and I vomited each morning. The grief ate at me from within and I thought my grief couldn't burrow any deeper.

I was wrong.

*   *   *

A month after my return to Sweden, I suddenly suffered from a severe pain in my lower abdomen. I was doubled up with cramps and the pain made me cry out. I didn't understand what was going on, but when I saw the blood flow down my legs the truth dawned on me.

Lost in my all-consuming grief, it didn't bother me that I hadn't had any periods and I was convinced that my morning sickness was due to my state of mind. I didn't realise that I was pregnant with Brian's child.

I'd had a miscarriage. My grief had killed our child, our eagerly awaited Johanna, who should have slept and played in Brian's blue room and crawled up into the bed in the mornings and woken Brian with the words he longed to hear:

'Daddy! Daddy! Wake up! I want to show you something!'

After my miscarriage, my grief doubled. I couldn't stop crying. My sense of guilt weighed me down. The anguish was unbearable.

I was convinced that I was going to die. It hurt so much. I suffered from cramps and thought I was going to choke. When the attacks were at their worst, I had to take a Valium to prevent myself from going crazy.

The week following the miscarriage is a blur. I only remember crying ... and crying ... and crying ...

I didn't want to go on. I wanted to be reunited with Brian and Johanna. My life was over. My loved ones were already on the other side and I ached to be with them. There was nothing left for me in this world.

I slipped progressively into the deepest of depressions and nothing was worth living for.

Or so I thought.

*   *   *

I'm not sure what happened, but I remember waking up one morning feeling the faintest glimmer of hope in my heart. My thoughts went out to Brian and Johanna. I know that Brian had always wanted the best for me and I admitted to myself that my mother was right. He would have been destroyed to have seen me like this.

The loss of Brian had made me mourn more deeply than I'd ever thought possible, but it was Brian who brought me back to life. I had to survive for his sake. I had to clear his name.

I don't know what happened that odd day, but I think I received help from above. From Brian.

Slowly, I started to eat again, and I left my room and took recuperative walks in the woods. I was still young and I was relatively healthy. After a few weeks, I'd recovered physically and felt stronger. I still grieved, but I had learned to live with my grief.

I suddenly felt a strong desire to go back to England, one which I couldn't resist. I wanted to meet people, talk to them, maybe even get in contact with the police. I had to try to reveal the truth surrounding Brian's death — for his sake, for his son's sake and for his parents' sake.

I couldn't continue knowing that the people Brian loved thought that he'd killed himself through his abuse of drugs and alcohol.

And something else spurred me on. Frank had to be punished before Brian could rest in peace. It was the least I could do for him.

I managed to convince my parents that I had to go back to London. It wasn't easy. They didn't think that I was strong enough. But I was determined and finally they gave in.

They even paid for my ticket.

CHAPTER SIXTEEN

THE BREAK-IN

BRIAN

My visit to Cotchford Farm was deeply upsetting. The empty, abandoned house and the glittering pool, where I'd held Brian in my arms for the last time, forced me to accept the truth. Brian was dead. He would never return to me.

I managed to pull myself together, glanced over at the pool and said goodbye to Brian.

'I will never forget you,' I whispered. 'You'll have a place in my heart for ever and I'll do my utmost to defend your name. I promise.

'I love you, Brian, and I hope that we'll be reunited some day.'

I blew a kiss to the swimming pool and turned round. I wanted to go into the house to see if Lewis was right. I found it hard to believe that the house had been stripped bare. I didn't want to believe the rumours I'd heard about a bonfire. Were there really people who hated Brian enough to dance on his grave? I couldn't and wouldn't believe it.

I wondered about how I could get into the house and remembered the dogflap, which was big enough for a Great Dane, in the kitchen door. It seemed the most obvious point of entry.

I crawled in and when I stood up in the kitchen the silence was shattered by a deafening alarm signal. It sounded almost as loud as an air-raid warning. It scared me and I ran to the door in the dining room and got out. I couldn't recall there having been an alarm there when Brian and I lived in the house. It must have been installed after his death.

I didn't know what to do. I stood in front of the door staring at the house, unable to move.

A few minutes passed and then I heard a familiar voice.

'Anna! Anna! My dear, dear child!'

Mrs Hallett and her husband came running down the driveway to see what was going on. Their cottage was just a few minutes from Cotchford Farm and I guessed that they'd heard the alarm.

When I saw Mrs Hallett I threw myself into her arms and started to cry again. She led me to the small slope in front of the swimming pool and we sat down on the grass.

'Anna, Anna,' she murmured and rocked me like a baby. 'My poor little girl.'

'Brian was killed,' I sobbed. 'He didn't drown. He was killed.'

'There, there,' Mrs Hallett said. 'Things will sort themselves out, just wait and see.'

Mrs Hallett rocked me in her arms until the police came. She explained who I was, but the policeman insisted that I should go with him to the station to leave my fingerprints. Once there, I bumped into the policeman who'd questioned me after Brian's death. He sat down beside me and put a comforting arm around my shoulder.

'Brian was killed,' I sobbed. 'He didn't just drown. You must do something.'

'I think I know what you're talking about,' the policeman said. 'But for your sake I think it's best that you leave things as they are. Try to get on with your life, Anna. You're young and strong. And even if you don't believe me, I know that you'll forget and move on.'

I had no choice. I'd done my best to clear Brian's name. The police didn't want to listen to me. But I felt in my heart that they knew I was right.

*　　　　*　　　　*

Thirty years have passed since Brian was killed.
The policeman was wrong.
I have still not forgotten.

EPILOGUE

BRIAN

After the upsetting visit to Cotchford Farm, I went back to London and did my best to try to get over Brian and our life together.

I threw myself into the nightlife of London and enjoyed myself in my favourite clubs: Revolution, The Speakeasy and Tramp. The only thing that mattered was drugs and rock 'n' roll. In that order. Nothing else. I tried hard to forget Brian, to push him from my mind. The drugs and nightlife were my way of escaping from the truth.

But one day I came to my senses. I realised that I couldn't continue with this destructive lifestyle. I had to pull myself together. I also felt that London had nothing to offer me but sad memories and grief.

During my stay in London, I'd got to know an American girl, Victoria, and we shared a flat together.

She'd often said that I should leave London and move to Los Angeles with her, and convinced me that I'd love her home town.

I also got to know Lawrence, who was a hairdresser and owned a saloon in New York. He was about to open a chain of new salons and invited me to come and stay with him in New York.

Late in the summer of 1970, I went back to Sweden to tell my parents about my new plans. After a while, Victoria joined me and stayed with me for three weeks, during which time we planned our new life in Los Angeles. Victoria left after we decided to meet up in the US before the end of the year.

But it wasn't to be.

During my stay in Stockholm, I went out with my friends and continued enjoying the nightlife. The rumours had spread, though, and everyone knew that I was the girl who'd lived with Brian Jones. It cut both ways. Some people understood my pain, others were mere sensation seekers and hurt me deeply by their insensitive comments. Everyone had formed their opinions of Brian and, with the exception of my closest friends, they were convinced that Brian had died a classic rock 'n' roll death. I tried not to listen and I refused to discuss Brian's death with any of them.

After a couple of months, a friend of mine introduced me to her boyfriend and a friend of his. This friend started to date me. He sent me flowers and chocolates and was always there for me. I was still vulnerable and it was nice to have someone taking care of everything. After two months of going out together, he asked me to marry him. I wasn't in love with him when we got married in December 1970, but I was swept away by the feeling that he wanted me and cared for me. The love came later.

We had a good life together over the next 25 years, dividing our time between our house in Sweden, our summer house in Spain and travelling around the world.

A little more than a year after our wedding, we had a daughter and my life changed for the better. She was everything I could have dreamt of and she completed my life. I named her Amanda after Amanda Lear, who'd been a close friend of Brian's.

My husband and I never talked about Brian. He was jealous of him and when we moved in together he tore my address book and my diary to pieces. He didn't want me to have any reminders of Brian. But I managed to save some clothes, my scrapbook with press cuttings and my treasured photograph of Brian as a young boy by hiding them at my mother's house. I couldn't bear to be parted from my only memories of Brian. They meant too much to me.

Throughout the years I was married, I tried my best to forget Brian. But there was always someone or something which reminded me of him. Years later, I understood that I had never allowed myself to grieve for my loss. Instead, I'd tried to repress my feelings and tried to convince myself that he'd never existed.

Brian was the first, but not the only love in my life. I eventually fell in love with my husband and we lived a comfortable family life for many years. Of course, we had our ups and downs, but it was important to me to have a family and I wanted to keep it together. But after 25 years, after our daughter had moved out, my husband and I drifted apart. He'd met someone else and when I finally found out, I moved into an apartment of my own.

For the following few months, I threw myself into redecorating and it wasn't until I'd finished that I realised what had happened. That feeling of loss and sadness was not new; I'd had the same feeling when I lost Brian.

The separation from my husband rekindled all the feelings of loss that I'd had when Brian died, and the grief hit me with such a force that I was doubled up with pain. It was a recurrence of the desperation I'd felt over Brian's death. I thought I was going out of my mind.

In retrospect, I think that for the first time, I allowed myself to grieve, and the grief was for both Brian and my husband. The separation allowed me to think about Brian without a feeling of guilt. I know that Brian has been with me over the years, but now I felt free to talk and think about him without having any guilty feelings because of my family.

And I was at last free to tell the truth about Brian's last few months and the life we'd had together, until the tragic night when I lost him for ever.

During all these years, I've had a strong feeling of guilt for not having stood up and told the world what really happened that night, and I also blamed myself for having left him in the pool with Frank. I don't know how many times I've asked myself how I could have done that. If only I'd ignored the mysterious first phone call, he would still be alive.

Today, I know that Brian's death wasn't my fault, and I also know that the only thing I can do is tell the truth once and for all. And that's why I've written this book.

Thirty years have past and I might have forgotten a thing or two, but this is my story and it's also a declaration of love for the man I loved so dearly when I was still a young woman.

While working on this book, I've also returned recently to Cotchford Farm and met the new owners, Alistair and Harriet Johns. I won't deny that I was a bit nervous when I got there. Over time, things have changed. The house where Frank used to stay was pulled down shortly after Alistair bought the farm and a new house was built in its place. The gravel drive down to the farm had also been altered. But the lovely house was exactly as I remembered it. It felt like coming home when I saw it.

I know that Brian would have approved of and liked the Johns family. He always wanted Cotchford Farm to be a lively home with lots of children and animals, and that's exactly what it is. Brian would also have been pleased with the way the family have looked after the house. They've made some changes, adding a modern kitchen and another entrance to the living room, the room we called the music room. In the garden, they have a smaller vegetable patch and the rose garden is gone. But the statue of Christopher Robin is still there, as well as the sundial with Winnie the Pooh and the other characters from Brian's much-loved books. And even though the pool brought back the sad memories of my last night with Brian, it is still beautiful.

As I strolled through the garden, I felt sure that Brian had kept an eye on the house which he'd come to love so dearly and where he'd wanted to spend the rest of his life with his family. And I'm sure that he's grateful that Alistair Johns became the owner and not someone who just wanted it as an occasional retreat.

During my visit, I also got the opportunity to see Mrs Hallett, who is still living in the little cottage a few minutes walk from Cotchford Farm.

When I saw her again, the memories came flooding back. She's my last link to Brian, she's the one who was there with us. And she's still a lovely lady with a big heart and a great sense of humour.

What I didn't know before I met Mrs Hallett again was how much she actually loved Brian. It wasn't until I stepped into her living room, and saw the walls decorated with beautiful pictures of Brian, that I realised the depth of her affection. She had both photographs and sketches. I'm sure she loved Brian like a son, and I know that Brian loved her with all his heart. She was like a mother to him and she was someone we both depended on. It was wonderful to see her again and embrace her one more time, and I sincerely hope I'll see her again before long.

Since the terrible events all those years ago, the place I've longed to visit more than any other is Brian's final resting place, since I wasn't there for the funeral. It was as I'd hoped, a beautiful stone and a well-kept grave, covered with lovely flowers brought in by friends and fans. It felt good knowing that so many people had loved him and still remembered him, but at the same time it was so sad that he'd died so young and left me and all those who loved him behind.

I wished I could show him my beautiful daughter Amanda and my two young grandsons Marcus and Lucas, and tell him that, in spite of everything, I've had a good life. But I'm sure he knows and I'm sure he's happy for me and can appreciate that at long last I summoned up the courage to tell the world what really happened. I know it was and is important to him to let everybody know that he didn't die of drugs and alcohol. He was not to blame for his drowning. He was killed.

I'm also sure that, at long last, he will rest in peace. With this book I've finally told the world the truth about Brian's last few months and his tragic death.

Just as he'd have wanted, and just as he'd have urged me to do.